# BRIEF ENCOUNTERS

## NOTES FROM A

## PHILOSOPHER'S DIARY

### ANTHONY KENNY

First published in Great Britain in 2018

Society for Promoting Christian Knowledge
36 Causton Street
London SW1P 4ST
www.spck.org.uk

*British Library Cataloguing-in-Publication Data*
A catalogue record for this book is available from the British Library

ISBN 978–0–281–07919–3
eBook ISBN 978–0–281–07921–6

1 3 5 7 9 10 8 6 4 2

Typeset by Fakenham Prepress Solutions, Fakenham, Norfolk NR21 8NL
Printed in Great Britain by TJ International

eBook by Fakenham Prepress Solutions

Produced on paper from sustainable forests

# BRIEF ENCOUNTERS

# Contents

# Contents

# Introduction

This book is not an autobiography: still less does it attempt to offer brief lives of the subjects of its various chapters. I have had an interesting life, but the interest derives not from anything I have done myself, but from the variety of people I have been lucky enough to know and work with. In succeeding chapters I hope to give an account of my interaction with them. This introductory chapter is intended to give a chronological summary of my own life, so that the reader can tell at what stage and in what capacity I was interacting with the various characters.

I was born in Liverpool on 16 March 1931, the son of John Kenny, an engineer on a steamship engaged in the banana trade, and his wife, Margaret (née Jones). Sadly, I have only fragmentary memories of my father. Not only was he continually at sea, but by the time I was two years old my parents' marriage had broken up, and my mother and I lived in the house of my widowed grandmother. My father's ship, *Sulaco*, was enrolled in the Merchant Navy, and in October 1940 it was sunk by a German submarine with the loss of almost the entire crew.

My schooling was strictly ecclesiastical. For two years I was educated by nuns of the order of La Sagesse in a Liverpool suburb, and for the next five I studied at the Jesuit school of Saint Francis Xavier in the centre of the city. My education was interrupted by periods of evacuation to the countryside to avoid the German bombs which were falling on Merseyside. At the age of 12, I entered Upholland college, the junior seminary of the Liverpool archdiocese, and remained there for six years. From there I moved to the English College in Rome to complete training for the priesthood. I was ordained a priest in 1955.

After ordination I undertook graduate studies in theology, writing a dissertation on religious language, which involved one year of study in Rome and one in Oxford. The year in Oxford expanded into two to allow me to write simultaneously a philosophical dissertation, which became my first published book, *Action, Emotion and Will* (1963) which, in a second edition, is still in print.

There followed four years as a curate in Liverpool, during which I became certain that my ordination had been a terrible mistake. Already, as a seminarian, I had felt doubts about aspects of the Catholic faith, but I stifled them. But before the four years were up, I had ceased to accept many of the doctrines that it was a priest's obligation to believe and teach. I decided to leave the priesthood and was laicized by Pope Paul VI in 1963. A year or two later I met my future wife, Nancy Caroline Gayley of Swarthmore, Pennsylvania, and we were married in 1966. We have two sons: Robert, born in 1968, and Charles, born in 1970.

Since 1964, my life has centred upon Oxford University. My academic discipline, once I had left the Church, was philosophy. At Oxford, philosophy is taught as one of several groups of disciplines making up BA courses known as 'honour schools'. The two principal ones were known as 'Greats', in which philosophy was combined with ancient history and literature, and 'PPE', in which it combined with politics and economics. After two terms in a temporary post shared between Trinity and Exeter colleges, I was elected to a tutorial fellowship at Balliol. Tutorial fellows of colleges form the backbone of Oxford's academic staff. As a member of a college's governing body, a fellow, however junior, shares, on equal terms, the administration of an ancient charitable corporation. If the fellow is also a tutor, he or she is responsible – perhaps with one or two colleagues – for the education of undergraduates in his or her own particular discipline.

When appointed to Balliol I was, as a matter of routine, made a Master of Arts of the university. This made me a member of Congregation, the assembly of all MAs engaged in teaching or administration in Oxford. Congregation was the town meeting of dons; in constitutional terms, it was the sovereign body of the university. Most of the university's executive business was conducted by a much smaller elected body, called Hebdomadal Council; but any proposed change in the university statutes, or major item of business, had to be submitted for approval to Congregation, which met several times each term.

An autobiography of my Oxford days would have for its most accurate title, *A Life in Committees*. For the first part of my career, these would be college committees, and in the latter part, university committees. In the course of time I served on most college committees, but my main administrative experience was as senior tutor for four years. The senior tutor was responsible for the academic administration of the college, and for arranging and monitoring the tutorial teaching of junior members.

I had not been senior tutor for long when, in April 1976, I was placed on the search committee to seek a new Master to replace Christopher Hill, who was retiring in 1978. After a year considering various outside candidates, the Balliol fellows decided that they wanted to elect a candidate from within the fellowship. At this point I withdrew from the search committee, and was myself chosen as Master in the spring of 1978. I took office in October of that year.

The Master of a college has little statutory authority. He or she chairs the governing body, and has a casting vote, but the only power he or she has is the power to persuade. In the course of a dozen years as Master I often had to cheerfully accept being voted down. In the last week of every eight-week term, the Master has to conduct an operation known as 'handshaking'. Undergraduates come, one by one, to sit at the dining table in the lodgings and listen to their subject tutors as they report to the Master on the term's work. Handshaking gives a head of house an opportunity to check up on the tutors as well as undergraduates.

In an autobiography, I described the job of a Master in these words:

A Master of Balliol has to relate to the three different estates of the college: the junior members, the senior members, and the old members. It is one of his duties to try to make each of these groups understand and be ready to learn from the others. I spent much of my time trying to explain to undergraduates why dons think as they do and to dons why undergraduates behave as they do, and to alumni why the college today is not what it was when they were in the heyday of their youth. If I were asked to put the duties of a Master in a nutshell I would say that it is to be a peacemaker: to hold the ring between senior and junior members, to persuade one fellow that he has not been impardonably insulted by another, and to reconcile old members to the college of the present day.*

A job description today, rather than in the heyday of student revolution, would place less emphasis on peacekeeping between junior and senior members. It would, however, lay stress on something not then mentioned: the raising of funds for the college. I did in fact, as Master, head a septcentenary appeal; but it took less than two years, and for most of my tenure I was allowed to direct my energies elsewhere.

Being Master gave me an opportunity to meet Balliol alumni who had gone into various walks of life: several of them figure in later chapters. Members from past years would reassemble from time to time in gaudies, and sometimes they would come to take a look at the college and decide whether to encourage their children to apply to it. One such visit was made by William Rees-Mogg, then the editor of *The Times*. He took one look at the college, and one look at me, and decided to send his son Jacob to Trinity.

One of my philosophical interests was in the area of overlap between philosophy and law. In order to make an honest lawyer of myself I joined Lincoln's Inn and sat Bar examinations during my last years at Balliol. I passed the academic stage, but was never called to the Bar because, not having any desire to practise, I did not take the practical examinations. However, in the course of time, Lincoln's Inn made me an honorary bencher.

In 1980 I was elected to Hebdomadal Council, an elected body of some two dozen members presided over by the vice chancellor which, in the 1980s, met weekly in term time to conduct the business of the university. I served on many committees: in particular, I was

---

* A. Kenny, *A Life in Oxford* (London: John Murray, 1997), p. 18.

a curator of the Bodleian Library, and chaired the Libraries Board, which funded nearly a hundred libraries across the university.

Having served as Master of Balliol for 11 years, I resigned. When first elected, I had been comparatively young, and therefore had stated that I would not hold office for more than 12 years. I was succeeded by Baruch Blumberg, an American Balliol alumnus who had won the Nobel Prize for Medicine. Barry was Jewish, but also a member of the Pontifical Academy of Sciences. He had no difficulty in adapting the Balliol grace – 'Benedictus benedicat' – into Hebrew as 'Baruch barucha',* and he placed himself with enthusiasm under the patronage of the Balliol patron saint, St Catherine of Alexandria.

St Catherine is best known for breaking the wheel on which she was to have been martyred. She was also the patron saint of philosophers, having defeated in argument the hundred sages who had been employed by the Roman emperor to convert her to paganism and matrimony. She often appears in art as espoused in childhood to the infant Jesus. Indeed, of all the saints other than the Virgin Mary, she has a claim to be the one most frequently represented in Western painting.

The only problem with St Catherine is that she did not exist. She was invented, perhaps in the sixth century, by the abbot of a convent in Sinai who found that the abbey's main relic, Moses' burning bush, was no longer attracting enough pilgrims. He, or one of his monks, devised the legend, and concluded with a miraculous transfer of the saint's body from Alexandria to Sinai. During my time at Balliol, Pope Paul VI, recognizing the fabulous nature of her biography, removed St Catherine's feast from the Church's calendar.

Barry Blumberg, having taken office as Master, regarded the saint's removal from the calendar as an insult to Balliol. He took the matter up with Pope John Paul II at a meeting of the Pontifical Academy. The pope told him that St Catherine had been removed only from the universal Church calendar and her feast could still be celebrated locally. Barry and I remained puzzled as to how she could

---

\* 'May the Blessed One give a blessing.'

exist in some places and not in others, but the college continues to celebrate her every 25 November. Barry's intervention must be the only time in history that a pope has been rebuked by a Jewish head of an Oxford college for an insult to the college's patron.

When I left Balliol, I became instead the Warden of Rhodes House, and Secretary of the Rhodes Trust, which was my employer for the next ten years. A Warden of Rhodes House, as I understood the job, has four main tasks: as Secretary of the Rhodes Trust, he or she is chief (and sole) executive officer of a charitable foundation that derives ultimately from the will of Cecil Rhodes. As International Secretary of the Rhodes Scholarship scheme, the Warden has to keep in touch with national secretaries who, in a score of countries, organize locally the selection of Scholars. Once the Scholars are selected, it is the Warden's task to place them in colleges and on courses in Oxford, and to provide their funding, monitor their performance and offer backup pastoral care during their time on stipend. Finally, the Warden is responsible for the upkeep and management of Rhodes House itself, which in addition to providing a residence and rooms for entertainment contains a number of grand ceremonial rooms which can be used for social and charitable purposes.

The trust at that time was governed by eight trustees, four from Oxford and four from London. The London trustees in my time included Lord Ashburton, Lord Armstrong of Ilminster, Lord Sainsbury of Preston Candover, and the Conservative cabinet minister William Waldegrave. As Warden, I was fortunate to be able to draw on the financial and political expertise thus represented. Without it, my task would have been impossible.

A few statistics will bring out some of the differences between being Master of Balliol and being Warden of Rhodes House. A Master must try to become acquainted with more than 500 Balliol men and women in residence at any time; a Warden, when I took over, had just over 200 Scholars to recognize and entertain. Each year a Master must chair nine governing bodies of sixty-odd fellows; a Warden, as Secretary of the Rhodes Trust, services annually three meetings of eight trustees. At Balliol, a Master is invited to attend, by my reckoning, some 260 committees a year; the Rhodes Trust has only one committee, and that does its business by circulation. The endowment income of Balliol in 1988–9 was £1,400,000; the endowment income of the Rhodes Trust in the same year was £4,900,000. A Master has to spend time seeking funds to increase the college's endowment; one of a Warden's duties was to distribute funds, at the behest of the trust, to institutions which solicit its aid. By the time I left Rhodes House the trust was worth almost £200,000,000, with an income approaching £6,000,000.

The prime charge on the assets of the trust was, of course, the upkeep of the scholarship scheme. I was fortunate to be Warden during a period of buoyancy on the stock market, and during my time the trustees greatly expanded the scholarship scheme. By the end of 1996, there was a record number of 247 Rhodes Scholars on stipend. After maintaining the scholarships, the trust usually had a substantial annual surplus to disburse on charitable purposes. Apart from educational causes in South Africa, the principal beneficiaries of the trust in the 1990s were the colleges and the University of Oxford.

My Rhodes job brought me into a new international circle of acquaintances. Shortly after I became Secretary of the Trust I was invited by the entrepreneur Algy Cluff to a party in honour of Robert Mugabe. The party was to encourage investment in Zimbabwe, and Algy must have hoped that the Rhodes Trust would put some of its funds there. The hope was not unrealistic because my predecessor as Warden, Sir Edgar Williams, had been a member of the delegation to Rhodesia that persuaded the British government to back Mugabe, rather than Bishop Muzorewa, as prime minister of the newly independent country. Mugabe, in those days, was soft spoken and gave an impression of great shyness. He gave a low-key speech of orthodox Marxist economics, and was followed by his finance minister who told us, in effect, not to worry about Comrade Mugabe's remarks: 'Gentlemen', he said, 'your money is safe with us.' But I did not recommend the trustees to take up the invitation to invest.

The Rhodes Scholars who came under my care while I was Warden were, almost without exception, gifted and charming. Sadly, because they are scattered in many countries, I have not been able to keep in touch with them in the way that I have been able to make occasional contacts with the British alumni of my Balliol period. Quite a number of the Scholars, though, have already risen to senior office. From America I think of Senator Cory Booker from New Jersey, Governor Bobby Jindal of Louisiana, and Ben Jealous, running for governor of Maryland. In Canada the foreign minister is Cynthia Freeland, who, while a Scholar, was already a leading correspondent of the *Financial Times*.

One Rhodes Scholar, who was already in Oxford determined to make his mark in the world, was Arthur Mutambara from Zimbabwe. Before coming to Oxford in 1991 he had been Secretary General of the University of Zimbabwe's Student Union, where he had fallen foul of the authorities for making provocative political statements. One evening at dinner with us in Rhodes House he was loud in voicing criticisms of the Mugabe regime. My wife took him aside: 'Be careful what you say, Arthur', she said. 'You don't know who is listening, and you don't want to find yourself put in prison when you get back to Zimbabwe.' 'Lady Kenny', he said, pulling himself up to his full height, 'when I get back to Zimbabwe it is going to be me who is putting people into prison.'

Sure enough, not many years after, Arthur became Deputy Prime Minister of Zimbabwe. This was when Morgan Tsvangirai of the Movement for Democratic Change was prime minister in an ill-fated Government of National Unity. Outmanoeuvred at the time by ZANU–PF, Arthur may yet have a political career in post-Mugabe Zimbabwe: we will watch with keen interest.

While I was Warden of Rhodes House I held a professorial fellowship at St John's College, which gave me a new set of colleagues and friends. Shortly after I arrived there the college gave a party to celebrate one of its alumni, Tony Blair, becoming prime minister. When I was introduced as an ex-Master of Balliol, Blair's response was, 'You turned me down for Balliol, which was my first choice to read law.' This was the first I knew of the matter, and of course it was not I, but the law tutors, who had rejected him. But I was amused that his rejection still rankled.

St John's was a richer and more conservative college than Balliol. Feasts were celebrated in grand style, with the toastmaster announcing: 'Mr President – I give you Church and Queen.' Recently I was told by a fellow who joined the college in the year of Queen Elizabeth's accession that when he first heard that toast he was sitting next to an elderly colleague who muttered, 'Thank God for that! I could never get used to saying "Church and King".'

In my last years at Balliol and my first years at Rhodes House I was a delegate of Oxford University Press (OUP). The Press is the publishing arm of the university and is one of the most important vehicles by which it carries out its educational mission. There are people in many parts of the world who know nothing of Oxford except its Press, and OUP's dictionary makers have brought the university as much prestige as any of its faculties.

The delegates form the committee which is responsible to the university for the running of the Press. In my day there were 16 of us, each chosen for expertise in a particular subject; we met, gowned, under the chairmanship of the vice chancellor on alternate Tuesday mornings in the Clarendon Building, the Press's original home. Our task was to approve a list of academic titles to go to contract. The actual work of commissioning, drawing up contracts, copy-editing, book production and marketing was of course the responsibility of professional publishers. But each subject editor worked closely with the relevant delegate, who saw all significant correspondence between editor, author and referees.

More significant than the delegacy itself is its finance committee. This is, in effect, the board of directors of a multimillion pound business with branches in many countries – the Press's American branch is bigger in its own right than any academic publisher in the USA. The finance committee had a very different ethos from the delegates meeting: the vice chancellor did not preside, no gowns were worn, and meetings were held not in the antique splendour of the Clarendon Building, but in a glossy office in the Press's new premises in Walton Street.

I was one of six delegates who sat on the committee. Alongside two outside members with business experience – Tim Rix and Martin Jacomb – we were in effect the non-executive members of the board, while the executive directors were the professional publishers who headed the different divisions of the Press. I was impressed by the way the Press maintained high academic standards while becoming ever more profitable. Every year it produced healthy annual surpluses which were used to assist the university – unlike most university presses in America which are subsidized by their parent bodies. In addition to supporting the university, OUP funded research projects on a substantial scale, such as the massive *Oxford Dictionary of National Biography* in 60 volumes, which was produced on time, and within budget, in 2005.

While the social and pastoral duties of the Warden of Rhodes House often intruded into the weekend, I found that the wardenship allowed me to also take on a London job for two days a week – first of all at the British Academy, then at the British Library. The British Academy is to the humanities and social sciences what the Royal Society is to the sciences. I had been elected to it in 1974, and from 1989 to 1993 I was its president. At that period, the Department of Education and Science had delegated to the Academy the provision of graduate scholarships to British students. As head of a body disbursing substantial government funds, I had to report from time to time to the Secretary of State for Education. During the Thatcher years, the office changed hands so often that I found it hard to keep count of successive secretaries: but I remember that of the ones I encountered, the least pompous and most efficient was Kenneth Clark.

Presiding over the Academy was my first experience of employing civil servants, and some of my decisions were unpopular with them. In order to decode their responses I had recourse to the former Cabinet Secretary, Robert Armstrong, who was one of my Rhodes trustees.

'Should I be troubled', I asked him, 'if they tell me that morale among them is now at an all-time low?'

'Don't worry', he told me, 'they say things like that all the time.'

'Suppose they say, "Would you mind giving me that instruction in writing?" What then?'

'Oh, in *that* case, perhaps you should think again.'

After I ceased to be President of the British Academy I joined the board of the British Library, and in 1993 became its chair. I now reported to the Secretary of State for National Heritage, and my favourite was Virginia Bottomley – though, in the course of one of her visits to the library, she nearly killed me. I asked her to demonstrate the operation of the library's new sliding shelves, and in particular the mechanism which ensured that no reader would be trapped when a pair of shelves slid together. The fail-safe device failed to be safe, and I had to shout 'Virginia' at the top of my voice to prevent being squeezed to death between two chunks of heavy metal.

My appointment to the British Library meant that I had to leave my position at Oxford University Press. I could foresee that my new post could give rise to conflicts of interest with great publishing firms. The British Library has the right to acquire a free copy of every book published in the UK, and this right of legal deposit is regarded by some publishers as burdensome. Moreover, one of my major tasks at the library was to try to arrange that the copyright privilege should be extended to publications in electronic rather than book form. This was eventually introduced into legislation, but only some years after my tedious negotiations with the publishers' representatives.

I found that my experience at the Oxford libraries board was helpful when I was at the British Library, in particular in connection with catalogue digitization. I was, for a while, a member of the advisory board of the Online Computer Library Center (OCLC), the vast international digital catalogue, based in Ohio. As the great catalogue in the sky it soon trumped DOBIS/LIBIS, the European consortium we had erroneously backed when modernizing the Bodleian catalogue. I also chaired the committee that organized the British National Corpus, a vast database of current written and spoken English.

After I retired from Rhodes House, at the end of the millennium, I was briefly re-employed by Oxford University and made president of the university's development campaign. I did not enjoy this job, was not good at it, and was glad when it was over. My successor, Tony Smith, told me that it should be an easy job: really rich people, he told me, were like cows with full udders, pleading to be milked. I hope that was how he found it – he was indeed a skilled fundraiser – but that was not at all my experience.

Once I retired, my wife Nancy, 12 years younger than me, became the main breadwinner. She had started our married life as a piano teacher and opera singer; now she found a new vocation in the service of Oxford University. Having been the lead amateur in assembling funds to build a university swimming pool, she turned professional and took charge of development for the Refugee Studies Centre. Later she switched to what she insisted was a quite distinct profession and became Head of Alumni Relations. Oxford was ahead of other universities in paying attention to its alumni, and Nancy soon became a leader of the profession nationally.

In parallel with my official postings I have enjoyed a career as a writer. Over a long life, I have published some 50 books on philosophy, religion, history and literature. Most of the titles are listed in a Festschrift compiled by my friends Peter Hacker and John Cottingham – *Mind, Method, and Morality* (OUP, 2010). My most substantial work was composed in retirement. After I left Rhodes House, Oxford University Press asked me to write a *New History of Western Philosophy* in four volumes. During the early years of the millennium, I submitted each year a volume of some 125,000 words. Eventually, in 2010, the entire history appeared in a single volume. Since then it has been translated into many languages, most recently Chinese and Romanian.

Two books that gave me great pleasure to work on were written in collaboration with my sons: one on happiness, published by Charles and myself in 2006, and one on the reform of Oxford, published by Robert and myself in 2007. Every one of my books has been read in draft by my wife, who has struck out many an ill-judged paragraph. She has placed my readers in her debt by saving them hours of unprofitable reading. For advice on the present book I am grateful to her, to Robert and Charles and their wives, and to Jill Paton Walsh.

Anyone who makes the mistake of reading this book as an autobiography may conclude that I have made friends only with academics and people in public office. This would be far from the truth. I have deliberately excluded from my dramatis personae the living members of my family and my closest personal friends. It is to them this book is dedicated.

*Anthony Kenny*

# 1

## Three priests

### Monsignor Alexander Jones, Scripture scholar

The man who had the most influence on my life was my maternal
uncle, Alec Jones. I did not meet him, however, until my third
year. At the time of my birth he was a 25-year-old student for the
priesthood at the Venerable English College in Rome, attached to
the Pontifical Gregorian University. Such a student was not allowed
home, and so in order to see him I had to be taken to Rome. My
mother and grandmother attended his ordination as a priest, while I
was parked with another seminarian in the college. During this visit,
Alec took us to see Pope Pius XI in a private audience. My conversation with the pontiff was restricted to telling him, when asked,
that I was two-and-a-half years old. (In later childhood I wondered
why he needed to be told – wouldn't he have known already, being
infallible?)

The Venerable English College had, at this period, two notable
characteristics: loyalty to the Holy See, combined with English
exceptionalism. Centuries of persecution – so the staff and students
believed – gave the heirs of English recusants an insight into the
essence of the Catholic Church unshared by Catholics in other
countries. The college gloried in the martyrdoms suffered by many
of its graduates in penal times, and saw as its ultimate aim to convert
England, so that all English men and women would become Roman
Catholics and accept the authority of the pope. In one letter home,
Alec wrote: 'If Protestant England knew what a spirit there is here
for the conversion of the country, it would shake in its shoes.'

In 1935, Alec returned from Rome to teach in the seminary of
the Liverpool archdiocese, a handsome sandstone college called
Upholland, standing in substantial grounds in a rural part of
Lancashire. From then onwards, he would spend every Saturday
with his mother and sister and me. My parents had separated

soon after I was born, and my father was killed in the Battle of the Atlantic. It was Alec who took the place of a father in my life. He lived with us during holidays, and he and I spent much time cycling in the Lancashire lanes (then, during wartime petrol rationing, almost free of motor cars). A high point was a cycling trip to Stratford-upon-Avon to see a week of Shakespeare plays at the Memorial Theatre (for which Alec had to get a special dispensation from the archbishop, since priests were not allowed to visit theatres). He became a great fan of the actress Margaretta Scott, who played Portia and Lady Macbeth. I can still hear the disappointment in his voice when he looked at the programme for Hamlet and whispered, 'Margaretta Scott's not in!'

At the age of 12 I decided that I wanted to become a priest, and joined the junior seminary at Upholland. My decision was, above all, an expression of admiration for my uncle. He was a person who, throughout his life, charmed everyone who met him, and it surprised no one when I decided that I wanted to follow in his footsteps. At Upholland, his main job was to teach Scripture in the senior seminary, to the divines in their early twenties. I was in the junior school, learning Latin, Greek and history, so it was many years before I actually sat at his feet in a classroom. But he would invite me up to his study at weekends and spoil me with various sweetmeats.

One paternal role which Alec declined to fulfil was that of imparting instruction about sex. Indeed, he sent me out of the room when, during our Stratford week, the guide to Shakespeare's birthplace offered to explain how it was that Anne Hathaway had a baby a few months after she married him. I remained ignorant of the nature of human reproduction until I was about 15. Then, one day during the vacation, I confessed to my Benedictine parish priest that I had sinned by reading a book on the Virgin Birth for an unworthy motive – namely, to discover the mechanics of birth and conception. The priest was not as shocked as I expected, and told me that since I had no father I should ask my mother to let me visit him outside confession and receive appropriate instruction. When I went to see him he began by saying, 'You will have noticed that when you see a pretty girl, the thing between your legs stands up.' This took me by surprise: that was not at all what I had come to talk about. But he went on to say, 'It is a key that fits a lock, and I will tell you what the lock is like and what it is for' – and then proceeded to explain the operation of sex in a concrete, but not at all prurient, manner.

As a teacher of Scripture, Alec was lively and, by the standards of the time, liberal. In collaboration with a Jesuit from the Biblical Institute in Rome, he wrote a solid textbook for schools entitled *The Kingdom of Promise*. He went on to write a series of articles on the Old Testament for the *Catholic Gazette*, concealing his learning under a light and sometimes knockabout style. The first article begins, 'Adam's apple has stuck in many a throat and wits have observed that it needs a pillar of salt to digest the "Whale" story.' The articles were eventually collected in a book entitled *Unless Some Man Show Me*, in allusion to Acts 8.27–31. The book sold well and led to invitations to lecture in three continents.

In one of the original articles, Alec had written that it was no part of Catholic doctrine that the whole human race was descended from a single pair. While we were on a family holiday we learned that Pius XII had just issued an encyclical, *Humani Generis*, in which this single descent was emphasized as an indispensable element of the creation story. Frantic efforts had to be made to recall the proofs to add a footnote to bring the text into accord with the papal directive.

When the time came for my own ordination, in 1955, Alec persuaded the Archbishop of Liverpool, the future Cardinal Godfrey, to go to Rome to ordain me and a colleague in a private ceremony in the villa of the English College on Lake Albano. Alec brought my mother out from England, and at my celebration of the Mass with the archbishop they led the queue up the altar steps to kiss my newly anointed hands.

In 1956, there appeared *La Bible de Jérusalem*, an annotated French version of the Bible produced by the École Biblique de Jérusalem. Alec was excited by its solid and open-minded scholarship, and decided to assemble a group of translators to render the text and the notes into English. Most of the contributors were seminary professors, but the team included J. R. R. Tolkien. Many of the collaborators fell by the wayside, and Alec himself had to take their place, ending up as the sole translator of 18 of the books, as well as editor of the entire enterprise. The *Jerusalem Bible* was eventually published in 1966. The task had stretched over ten years, far beyond the time he had estimated, or the £1,000 he had been paid by the publishers.

When the work began, Alec was still Prefect of Studies at Upholland. In 1961, Archbishop Heenan of Liverpool moved him to become chaplain of the Diocesan School for the Blind. The duties were light, and left more time for work on the Bible, but Alec felt cut off from the academic community that had been his home for 25 years. He suspected that the new archbishop had been glad to remove from the seminary a Scripture professor he regarded as too liberal.

Alec spent day after day alone in his study, surrounded by a dozen versions of the Bible stacked on an enormous semicircular bookrest he had had specially constructed. The structure formed a kind of pen around the desk, within which he huddled over a typewriter, wrapped in an ancient Roman cloak or *zimarra*.

By the time the *Jerusalem Bible* was published, I had left the priesthood and married. Alec was saddened by my defection, but was always sympathetic and particularly helpful in soothing my mother's discontents. He helped to officiate at my wedding in Swarthmore Pennsylvania, and became immensely devoted to my wife, Nancy. When, in the year after our marriage, I took a sabbatical leave at the University of Chicago, he stayed in our apartment while on a tour of the USA for the launch of the American edition of the *Jerusalem Bible*.

Shortly after he returned from his tour he was diagnosed with cancer, but after the removal of a kidney he was able to resume academic life at Christ's College, Liverpool. This, his last teaching post, was a happy environment for him, and a building there has been named after him. In 1969, his cancer returned, with secondary tumours on the brain. After a period as a difficult invalid he became calmer and bore with dignity, and even serenity, the loss of his strength and the fading of his wit. My wife's family as well as my own mourned his loss, and her father painted a posthumous portrait of him which captured wonderfully the sparkle of his smile. To this day it hangs over the table where we eat most of our meals.

## Monsignor Jack Kennedy, Rector of the English College in Rome

The longest friendship of my life was with Jack Kennedy. It lasted from the day in 1943 when I joined him in Low Figures (the second lowest class) in the junior seminary at Upholland, until the day of his death in 2016. We were brought together, initially, by inverted snobbery. I was the son of a school secretary; he had parents who managed and owned a prosperous fish and chip shop. This put us at the top of the social strata among the young Liverpool seminarians. We were both regarded as having posh accents. Jack, indeed, was alleged to have introduced himself on arrival as 'I am an Emmanuel man.' What that meant, or if it ever occurred, I have never known. But the nickname 'Manny' stuck to Jack for seven years.

We were also, intellectually, at the top of the class together. But there was a huge difference between us: I was hopeless at any kind of sport, whereas Jack was the best footballer and the best cricketer of the year. Only at tennis could I compete with him in any way, and the rare occasions when I beat him manifested his magnanimity rather than any skill of mine.

Throughout his life, Jack loved a bet. During one summer term he suggested that we should both read the novel *Ben-Hur*. He bet that he would finish first; the loser was to give up playing cricket for the term. The bet caused consternation among the sportsmen, since Jack was captain of the team and I was, at best, twelfth man. Cheered on by our classmates, Jack won by a chapter or two, and I was banned from the pitch. Jack relented after a while and allowed me to fumble my way through the last couple of matches of the term.

It was during our last two years at Upholland that Jack and I were closest. After we had passed School Certificate examinations in Latin and Greek, he and I, and one other, were exempted from classwork and left to study alone, apart from weekly composition tutorials in Greek and Latin prose. We were encouraged to draw up our own reading lists among the classical authors, and once the list had been approved we were on our honour not to make undue use of translations. All we had to do was to make notes on our reading and, in due course, discuss it in a tutorial. In this way, by the time we left Upholland, we had read together, sitting alone in the vast and empty study hall, many of the greatest works of Greek and Latin literature.

At the end of our years at Upholland, Jack and I were selected from among the sixth-formers to continue our studies at the English College in Rome. We travelled out together, taking our time, and sharing our first glimpses of the Winged Victory of Samothrace at the Louvre, the tragic Lion of Lucerne, the roof of Milan cathedral, and the mosaics of San Marco in Venice.

Once arrived in the Eternal City, Jack adapted to Italian cuisine faster than I did, and he introduced me to a Neapolitan delicacy that was then quite rare in Rome – the pizza. During our seven years in the college we were less close than we had been at Upholland. Jack was a winger in the games against Rugby Roma, and captained the cricket team which regularly played against the British Embassy at Palazzola. I became addicted to rock climbing and would take my vacations in the Apennines, the Alps or the Dolomites, while Jack preferred urban vacations. I cannot recall us ever taking a holiday together during our Roman years.

At the English College, we were fortunate to have the opportunity of viewing the latest films shortly after release, using copies that had been sent to Rome for dubbing into Italian. Jack was given the job of censoring the films for seminary use. Thus, for instance, many of the most exciting appearances of Sophia Loren fell to the cutting floor under Jack's scissors. But he was left with a lifelong admiration for her and, late in life, loved to tell the story of how, travelling on a first-class flight through the good offices of his brother (by then a director of British Airways), he found himself sitting next to the diva herself.

In 1955, Jack and I were both ordained priests, and a year later we completed our seven-year training. Once we graduated, Jack returned to England to serve as a curate in Wigan, while I returned to Rome for a year's further studies, followed by a period in Oxford. When I was laicized, Jack was much distressed, but it made no breach in our friendship, which continued until his death in 2016.

After serving in three different parishes, Jack was appointed to teach at Christ's College, Liverpool, where Alec had ended his days. He remained there happily from 1968 to 1984. In 1979 he took a sabbatical and enrolled on an MPhil programme in Oxford. After living for a while with the Jesuits at Campion Hall he came to live in The King's Mound, our Balliol residence. His charm quickly bewitched our young boys, whom he teased unmercifully. One day he asked our young son Charles, 'What was the worst name your daddy has ever called your mummy?' Charles found it difficult to recall any genuine memory of abuse, and had to take refuge in creative imagination. His eventual response was 'piggy-wiggy'.

In 1984, Jack became Rector of the English College. He was, inevitably, popular with the students, but did not have a trouble-free rectorship: at one time he had to cope with the problems of a homosexual coterie among the students. Moreover, his frank and candid manner in discussion made him at least one enemy in the Roman Curia. The upshot was that when his rectorship came to an end he did not go on to become a bishop, as most of his predecessors had done. Jack ended his clerical career as a parish priest in Southport.

He rendered valuable service to the national Church, however. At the height of the scandal over paedophile priests, he was a member of the committee – set up under Lord Nolan – to provide remedies and safeguards for the future. Jack's bluff common sense and ability to see through cant was a great asset to the committee.

Reluctant to leave his parish when he reached retirement age, Jack offered to let his curate take over as parish priest, and remain himself as a curate. Neither his bishop nor any of his friends thought this would be a credible arrangement, and he entered a clerical retirement community until, after a stroke, he needed permanent care.

In his last years he took several holidays in Italy with our family and charmed our granddaughters as he had charmed our sons. One of my fondest memories of Jack is of the two of us watching the sun go down over the Tuscan hills as we took turns in reading Dante to each other.

At Jack's funeral in Southport I was asked to speak, and since I was following two senior clergymen I took it that my role was to stress the lighter side of his life. I found that all my best lines – about his relationships with bookmakers, for instance – had been stolen by the earlier speakers. That was sad, because the funeral orations, collectively, did not do justice to the down-to-earth piety and pastoral concern that had been the centre of his life.

## Herbert McCabe, Dominican theologian

When I went to Oxford in 1957 as a graduate student – still a priest – Jack Kennedy gave me an introduction to a Dominican at Blackfriars, Herbert McCabe, who had been a university friend of his elder brother Frank. I soon found that Herbert was one of the most interesting people to discuss philosophy with, not only by comparison with other Catholics but by comparison with anyone in the university. He was a man of extremely sharp intelligence, and there is no doubt that if he had chosen to pursue an academic career he could have become one of the most distinguished philosophers in the country.

Born to a Catholic family in Middlesbrough in 1926, and baptized John Ignatius, McCabe studied philosophy at Manchester in the 1940s. He was taught by Dorothy Emmet, and was one of a group of student friends who went on to distinction in various fields – Robert

Bolt as a dramatist, Frank Kennedy as a diplomat, Robert Markus as a historian, Alasdair MacIntyre as a philosopher. Instead of pursuing a secular career, in 1949 he joined the Dominican Order of Preachers, taking, as a friar, the new name Herbert, by which he was known for the rest of his life.

It is hard, indeed, to imagine Herbert as a conventional faculty member, and had he not become a Dominican his career might well have been bohemian rather than academic. But he was not a conventional friar, either, even if to some of his friends he came to embody the ideal of what a twentieth-century Dominican should be. He always acknowledged a great debt to the Dominicans, who taught him theology prior to his ordination in 1955. From them he acquired a close familiarity with the works of Thomas Aquinas, a rare and precious thing in a period when most Catholic students of philosophy and theology were fed on second-hand manuals of Thomism.

Besides a love of Aquinas, membership of the Order of Preachers gave much to Herbert to which only his fellow Dominicans are in a position to testify. So loyal was he that he was willing to defend some of the less popular features of the Order's history. He once wrote that in the Europe of its time, 'the Spanish Inquisition seems to have been a shining light of rationality, gentleness, and sanity' in respect of the use of torture. He was very fond of hitch-hiking, saying that it was the most appropriate form of transport for a mendicant (i.e. begging) friar.

Despite his lifelong passion for the thought of St Thomas, McCabe hated to be called a Thomist, and his own spoken and written presentations of the saint's teaching bore a highly personal mark. He only rarely provided textual documentation for the ideas that he credited to Aquinas, yet his exposition has a ring of authenticity often lacking in commentators of a more scholarly bent.

Apart from the Bible and Aquinas, the greatest influence on McCabe's thought was that of the later Wittgenstein. He sought to graft the insights of the twentieth-century thinker on to those of the thirteenth-century thinker, not out of a desire to appear up to date

– he showed no inclination to endorse any of the trendy intellectual fashions of the age – but because he recognized a genuine affinity between the two masters. The two philosophers present a vision of human beings as intelligent bodily agents that is far removed from the dualisms or physicalisms characteristic of the ages that separate them in time. Herbert brought out that Aquinas and Wittgenstein shared a conviction that it is through an unconstrained attention to the operation of language that we achieve philosophical understanding. But his own Aquinas is, as he admits, in a sense more linguistic than the historical Aquinas was. Whereas Aquinas himself undoubtedly believed that every thought we have can, in principle, be expressed in language, he did not, McCabe says, fully grasp that human thought just *is* the capacity to use language: '*We* analyse understanding and thinking in terms of human communication, whereas *Aquinas* analyses communication in terms of understanding and thinking.'

From time to time, Herbert and I gave joint seminars on the philosophy of religion, he arguing for theism and I for agnosticism. Many of our most fertile encounters took place in the public bar of the King's Arms, Oxford, where Herbert was a regular visitor. He was a brilliant preacher and lecturer, but was in no rush to publish, and most of his work has been published posthumously. In 1987, however, he did offer a collection of lectures, papers and sermons under the title *God Matters*. It treated Catholic doctrines in a highly individual style. His regular practice, when expounding a doctrine, was first to state it in a way that would seem familiar to both to those who accept it and those who reject it, then to deny that the doctrine – stated in those familiar terms – is true, and finally to urge that such a denial is not only compatible with, but essential to, the underlying Christian tradition.

Take, for example, the thesis that the Trinity is the mystery of three persons in one God. In his essay 'Aquinas on the Trinity', McCabe maintained that for Aquinas, the Trinity is hardly more mysterious than the plain existence of God. When we talk of God at all we do not know what we are talking about; we do not have even a rough idea what God is. Moreover, if we use 'person' in its modern English sense, we have no warrant for saying there are three persons in God – because in the Trinity there are not three distinct centres of consciousness. Instead of speaking of 'God the Father' we could as well speak of 'God the parents': the plural 'parents' would be no more misleading than the gender connotation of 'Father'.

Or consider the essay in which Herbert discussed petitionary prayer: 'Here is God just about to make it rain for the sake of the farmers and their crops in the fields around Clyst Honiton when he overhears the urgent prayer of the vicar who is running his garden party that afternoon and changes his mind.' Of course God cannot be manipulated in this way, so what is the point of asking for things in prayer? Aquinas' answer, he says, is that we should not say, 'In accordance with my prayer, God wills that it should be a fine day', but rather, 'God wills that it should be a fine day in accordance with my prayer.' God brings about my prayer just as much as he brings about the fine day. Prayer is not a means of getting anything done: it is, he said, a real absolute waste of time. But that does not mean we should not pray: it is a form of spiritual play.

Herbert's account of central Christian doctrines seemed surprising, perhaps even shocking, to some believers. At one point in his book he makes ironic reference to the possible presence of heresy hunters in his audience. In fact, he always took great pains to avoid heresy (more so than is obvious on the surface). Whether or not these efforts were always successful I do not pretend to judge.

Some saw Herbert as being in the tradition of the Catholic writers of the early twentieth century. In his admiration for St Thomas, and in his constant employment of paradox, he resembled G. K. Chesterton, though his Aquinas was very different from G. K.'s. Just as Hilaire Belloc revelled in the celebration of wine, Herbert liked to evoke the beauty of Guinness and Irish whiskey. He always loved to point out that when, after Pentecost, the Apostles were accused of being drunk, St Peter instead of saying 'we are teetotallers', said, 'Nonsense, it's only nine o'clock in the morning.'

If you went to a sermon by Herbert, you knew you were in no danger of falling asleep: his style as a preacher was at the furthest possible remove from the bland truisms one hears so often from the pulpit. One of his favourite devices was to take some ecclesiastical commonplace – such as 'the Church welcomes sinners' – and spell out what it meant, freed of cant: 'People who are really welcome to the Catholic Church are the murderers, rapists, torturers, sadistic child molesters, and even those who evict old people from their homes.' It was for such people, he said from the pulpit, that the Church existed: but he went on to admit, with a certain show of reluctance, that many of his congregation, perhaps even a majority, did not come into any of these categories.

# 2

# Three cardinals

## William Theodore Heard, Dean of the Holy Roman Rota

Students in the English College were encouraged to take as their confessors priests who were not members of the college's own staff. In my time, there were two such resident in the college: Father H. E. G. Rope, a lexicographer with the *Oxford English Dictionary*, who had come to the priesthood late in life, and Monsignor W. T. Heard, who was a judge ('auditor') of one of the Vatican courts – the Rota. I chose the latter as my spiritual director, and made my confession to him on average once a week.

Heard was a Scot, the son of a headmaster of Fettes, who had brought him up in a manner old-fashioned even at the end of the nineteenth century. He had gone to Balliol in 1911 and obtained a third in law and a rowing blue. Having converted to Rome he became a priest, and went on to spend almost all of his career in the Vatican legal hierarchy. When I knew him he was both an auditor of the Rota, deciding cases of marriage annulment, and a member of the Sacred Congregation of Rites, who adjudged candidates for canonization to sainthood. He told me that he dealt with annulments in the morning and canonizations in the afternoon – that was the more congenial order of judgements, since even those who failed sainthood had at least tried to be good.

Canonization procedures were arduous: helping once to clear his room I found seven volumes of argument devoted to two words of Maria Goretti, eventually canonized as a martyr to chastity. Her last words were 'Si, si'. Were these words reinforcing her previous rejection of her would-be seducer, with the words 'Dio non vuole' ('God does not will it')? Or were they a last-minute surrender to his proposition, too late to ward off the knife that took her life?

Heard rarely appeared in the college hall: his health permitted only a spartan diet, and it often appeared as if he kept alive on grissini and whisky. He lived on a separate corridor in a quiet corner of the building, where he shared a bathroom with Father Rope. The two elderly clergymen sometimes indulged in undignified quarrels about who had left the bathroom tap running, or who had flushed the toilet inefficiently, and the rector of the college would have to intervene to keep the peace. But for us youngsters who took him as a spiritual counsellor, Heard was something of an oracle, and we took his advice on many issues. My uncle Alec was alarmed at my choice of guru. During his own time in Rome in the thirties, he told me, a fellow student had consulted Heard about his aunt's problems with her teeth: 'Only one solution', Heard had told him. 'Have them all out at once.' The student passed on the message, and his aunt took the advice. When the student reported this proudly to Heard, the response was, 'Had all her teeth out? Worst thing she could possibly do.'

It was largely on Heard's advice that I persisted in my intention to proceed to ordination, in spite of recurrent worries about my vocation and doubts about the faith. Once I was a priest, I became quite a friend of his, and he was generous to me, lending and giving me many books and often asking me to his room for a nightcap. Once, when I complained to him about the shortage of modern French theology in the university syllabus, he gave me £2,000 to spend on books of my choice for the college library.

It was not until after I left Rome, and towards the end of my time as a priest, that Heard was made a cardinal and became Dean of the Rota and head of the papal judiciary. The Second Vatican Council was now in full swing, and I wrote a letter to him, hoping for some gossip. But his reply, after some kind expressions of concern about my own welfare, ended with the two sentences, 'Being boxed up in the Council for four hours a day I don't have any news. I am now doing a refresher course in theology so as to know rather more about it when the Council reopens.'

After I had left the priesthood and become a fellow of Balliol, the college decided to commission Derek Hill to paint a portrait of Heard, whom it had elected to honorary fellowship. At the party to present the portrait and hang it in the hall, the cardinal affected not to recognize me and would turn his back whenever I tried to join a group of fellows talking to him. He was the only one of my clerical friends to snub me after my laicization. The portrait hung in the hall until five years after Heard's death in 1973. The fellows then displaced it, and I hung it in the lodgings while I was Master, and borrowed it to hang in Rhodes House when I moved there.

## John Carmel Heenan, Cardinal Archbishop of Westminster

When I entered the English College in Rome in 1949, John Carmel Heenan was still remembered there, even though it was 18 years since he had departed. He was well known not so much for his current energetic evangelizing as a priest of the Catholic Missionary Society, but as the author of comic songs which he had written while a student, and which were still sung in the 1950s. The students of the college used to spend the months of July to September at Palazzola, a delightful villa in the Alban hills, away from the torrid heat of Rome. The villa had been a Cistercian monastery, and later a home for alcoholics, before it had been bought for the English College by Arthur Hinsley in the 1920s. On the last night of the vacation we would chant the farewell song that Heenan had written years before:

> I leave Palazzola with a tear in my eye,
> The villa's been lovely in spite of the pi,
> And though I like swotting and bricking in Rome,
> I prefer Palazzola, the inebriate's home.

I first encountered Heenan when he came to give us seminarians one of our twice-yearly three-day retreats. His addresses – 'conferences' we called them – were brisk and lively: the substance of them was later published in a book called *The People's Priest*. As I remember them, they did not contain any profound spirituality, but were full of sound practical advice on the administrative, not to say managerial, aspects of the priesthood. During the course of his visit I made my confession to him, but I cannot now recall either what sins I confessed or what, if any, spiritual advice he gave me.

It was six or seven years before we saw each other again. In 1951, Heenan became Bishop of Leeds, where he gained a reputation as an uncompromising reformer, a rebuker of idleness among the clergy, who nicknamed his diocese The Cruel See. In 1955, I was ordained as a priest of the Liverpool archdiocese by Archbishop Godfrey. A year later, Godfrey moved to Westminster, and Heenan became my archbishop. He accepted Godfrey's arrangement that I should spend a year in Oxford working on a doctoral thesis – on linguistic analysis and the language of religion – that was due to be submitted to the Gregorian University in Rome; but he discovered that if I enrolled also for an Oxford degree I would have my fees paid by the Liverpool local authority, and be given, in addition, a grant for living expenses. I would have to spend an extra year in Oxford, but he reckoned that two years at no cost to the archdiocese was better than one for which the archdiocese would have to pay. So I began working on two doctorates simultaneously.

Having completed my Gregorian thesis, but not my Oxford one, I left the university in 1959. Heenan wrote to me:

> I have given a great deal of thought to your future and I think that from every point of view it will be best if you have a year or two in a busy city mission. You will have a great deal to offer in years to come and I am sure that if you have some pastoral work as a foundation you will be better able to use your knowledge later on. Your time at Oxford will have been a benefit not only to you but to the Catholics at Oxford. But I am sure that in the immediate future you will benefit spiritually by working in a parish.

So for two years I was a curate in the parish of Sacred Heart, Hall Lane, in a run-down part of Liverpool. Heenan was anxious, however, that I should have an intellectual task as well as pastoral duties. He knew that I had an interest in English Catholic history, and had published a number of articles on the topic. Accordingly, he arranged for me to be a temporary archivist in the diocesan offices, which were within walking distance of my presbytery. Working in the same building he and I saw each other from time to time, and he would chat about his intention to scrap the existing plans for a mammoth Liverpool cathedral and to set up a competition calling for a more modest design.

The task Heenan gave me, however, was an embarrassing one. He had heard that the Nazis in Germany had ransacked the archives of dioceses to find papers that could be published to discredit the Church. He was anxious to prevent anything of the kind happening in England, so he asked me to go through the records and get rid of any stories of clerical misdeeds that were capable of being used for propaganda purposes. I could not refuse point blank an order from my archbishop, but it seemed to me wrong for an archivist to destroy, on such a partisan basis, material of historical interest. I compromised by separating embarrassing material into a special section which could, in the unlikely event of a hostile raid on the archives by some anti-clerical group, easily be destroyed.

However, I can testify that Heenan was not the heartless apparatchik depicted by many of his critics. During my time as a curate in Liverpool I fell into disfavour because I several times attacked, in print, the British government's policy of nuclear deterrence. I failed to persuade the archbishop of the immorality of the policy, and eventually he forbade me to write in diocesan publications. During one of our discussions I recall saying to him, 'Episcopacy corrupts, and archiepiscopacy corrupts absolutely.' (A remark of which, I regret to say, I was at the time rather proud.)

Later in life, as Master of an Oxford college during the years of student revolt, I had my own experience of dealing with bright and bumptious young men who were confident that they were in possession of the moral high ground. I cannot recall any of them ever being as rude to me as I had been to Heenan, yet he continued to exhibit a benevolent, and indeed generous, care for my welfare. For instance, he contributed substantially to the Catholic Housing Aid Society (a charity to help the poor get on to the housing market) of which I had founded a local branch.

After two years as a curate in central Liverpool, I fell ill with infective hepatitis. When I recovered, Heenan considerately moved me to a more salubrious parish in the suburb of Great Crosby. Still anxious that I should have intellectual as well as pastoral duties, he asked me to give religious instruction to the sixth-formers in the nearby grammar school of St Mary's. The idea was not well inspired. The Christian brothers who ran the school were outraged by the suggestion that they were insufficiently capable of giving instruction in the Catholic faith, and I was too inexperienced to keep under control a group of teenagers who obviously felt they already had more than enough teaching on religion. They passed the time pleasantly enough by teasing me with questions such as, 'What is the pope's attitude to sex change?'

For years I have put the embarrassing sessions in the classroom out of my mind, but was recently reminded of them from an unexpected quarter. At a reception in Westminster I was introduced to the present cardinal, Vincent Nichols. 'Your Eminence', I said, 'I don't think we have met before'. 'Oh yes we have', he replied, 'you taught me religion in the sixth form at St Mary's, Crosby.'

In 1963, the time came when I had to tell Archbishop Heenan that I wished to leave the priesthood because I could no longer believe many of the things that it was a priest's duty to teach. When I told him my story, he was friendly and understanding, offering neither exhortation nor rebuke. But he suggested that rather than being laicized immediately I should live in Rome for a while, and consult my former Jesuit supervisor, Bernard Lonergan. The second session of the Vatican Council was just beginning, and bishops needed theological advisers. No one thought it odd if bishops sent their clerics off to live in hotels in the holy city, so I spent a month in a pensione on the Via Nomentana at the archbishop's expense, imagined by many to be his theological adviser.

Soon after I arrived in Rome, Heenan was promoted to the see of Westminster, vacated by the death of Cardinal Godfrey. When he arrived in Rome to attend the Council, he invited me to see him in the English College. There he tried to persuade me that rather than being laicized I should take off my collar and earn my living for a few years as a layman; if my faith rekindled, I could then rejoin the priesthood. He also urged me to go and see the Abbot of Downside, who, he told me, was intelligent, holy and wise: 'He would understand you, and he would have plenty of time; good men always have plenty of time.' Heenan himself had given me plenty of time, but at a further meeting I convinced him that the halfway-house arrangement he had suggested would not serve. I returned home to Liverpool, and Pope Paul VI eventually released me from the priesthood at the beginning of the following January.

The Second Vatican Council was a turning point in Heenan's life. Forever loyal to successive popes, he found uncongenial the direction in which many of the Council fathers wished to take the Church. His distaste for academic theology found expression in speeches attacking the experts, or *periti*, who came from monasteries, seminaries or universities: he saw them as ignorant of 'the real world'. For him, theology consisted in an unquestioning acceptance of Vatican dictates, even if that meant – as in the case of the morality of contraception – a reversal of his own considered opinion on the topic. And for him, the worst sin was 'giving scandal' – that meant doing anything that showed the Church in a bad light, even if it was a true light. This laid up trouble for his archiepiscopal successors.

At Westminster, Heenan was uncomfortable in implementing the reforms initiated by the Council – the revision of the liturgy, the empowerment of the laity, the ecumenical approach to the separated Churches. His last years were saddened by the defection of so many of his priests, especially figures of the clerical intelligentsia – Charles Davis, Peter de Rosa, Hubert Richards and others. Meeting my uncle Alec on one occasion, Heenan said, 'The path that Tony trod has now become a great high road.'

Christopher Butler, the Abbot of Downside who had been so highly praised to me in 1963, eventually became an assistant bishop in Westminster. Butler came to look upon the cardinal as a classical figure of tragedy – a man of many virtues brought low by a single debilitating fault, namely, the arrogant clericalism that he well described in a letter to Hubert Richards:

He thinks (almost unconsciously) of the faithful as a crowd of unedu-cated East Londoners of the first decade of this century; and any lay person who shows more than a purely passive acceptance of the penny catechism is, for him, a tiresome person who does not under-stand his proper position in the Church.*

## Cormac Murphy-O'Connor, Cardinal Archbishop of Westminster

During my time at the English College a whole tribe of Murphy-O'Connors passed through the seminary. The eldest was Pat, three years my senior, then there was Brian, a year behind him, and finally Cormac, who was a year below me. In my early days in the college, Pat was my best friend. A weighty presence on the soccer and rugger field, a gifted singer and actor, a genial comic and mimic, Pat was the life and soul of any social event. He was a keen alpinist, and taught me rock climbing on some practice cliffs above Lake Albano which we named Jock's Tooth (after the college rector) and Ropey's Head (after the college confessor). Pat had a beautiful baritone voice, and I have golden memories of a summer villa performance of *The Gondoliers*, in which I sang and danced as a contadina while Pat took the lead part of the gondolier Giuseppe Palmieri.

When Cormac first appeared in college he was seen very much as a Murphy-O'Connor baby brother. He had an endearing innocence, which brought out the protective instinct in those of us senior to him. As he relates in his autobiography, in his early days in the college I taught him some tricks of Roman life, such as how to gatecrash a Vatican ceremony without a ticket. It was only after Pat left the college that Cormac – who was no less adept at sport – could be appreciated in his own right, rather than as a junior version of his elder brother.

As time went on, however, the young Cormac was the member of the family to whom I became closest. He was even more musical than

---

* J. Hagerty, *Cardinal John Carmel Heenan* (Leominster: Gracewing, 2012), p. 277.

Pat, and played the piano very sensitively. In our annual Gilbert and Sullivan performances he was more likely to be an accompanist than a performer. Like his elder brother, Cormac was a keen climber, and one summer we ascended Monte Rosa, on the border between Italy and Switzerland. This involved sleeping in a refuge which was the highest in Europe, but the ascent was an easy snow climb and we did not need a guide. In his recently published memoir, *An English Spring*, Cormac recorded with affection our climb, and went on to say:

> We then endeavoured to climb the rock face of the Rothorn. A lightning storm suddenly descended upon us; the guide got thoroughly alarmed, and told us to throw away our ice axes. With lightening striking the rocks where we were stranded, I have rarely, if ever, felt so frightened. It might well have been the end of me and Tony. Thus would the world have been deprived not only of a future cardinal but, rather more important, one of the best English philosophers of the past fifty years.

I am glad that Cormac had such vivid memories of our time together in the Alps, and I am complacent about the flattery. The problem is that I have no recollection whatsoever of the dramatic events he described. After some reflection, I have decided that this is more likely due to a defect of memory on my part than to an excess of imagination on the cardinal's. I do recall that on our return to Rome after our Monte Rosa expedition the two of us ran out of cash. We had just enough left to pay for the train fare from Bologna to Rome, but to get to Bologna there was no alternative to hitch-hiking.

Before doing so, we had a long discussion as to whether we should wear our cassocks while thumbing lifts. Doing so would probably increase our probability of being picked up – but on the other hand, would it not give a false impression that we were engaged on some pastoral mission? Though I recall the discussion, I cannot remember what we eventually decided to do. My memory of it has vanished along with the nightmare on the Rothorn.

Cormac was ordained a year after me, and once he had returned to England we went our separate ways, though our friendship survived my leaving the priesthood and the Church. In 1971, he became Rector of the English College, and I was always welcome as a visitor there during his rectorship. My wife and I were invited to his enthronement as Bishop of Arundel and Brighton in 1977, and in the succeeding Christmas vacation my whole family were entertained by him in the episcopal palace – our boys' first encounter with a bishop.

Though my leaving the Church distressed Cormac, he never rebuked me or urged me to return to its fold. Recently, however, when Pope Francis' encyclical *Amoris Laetitia* appeared, I praised to Cormac the chapter of advice to couples on how to keep love alive within a marriage: 'Nancy and I', I told him, 'have long been doing what the pope says one should do.' A twinkle came into his eye: 'It's high time, Tony', he said, 'that you began to do what the pope tells you to do.'

As Archbishop of Westminster, Cormac became the spokesman for the Roman Catholics of England. In interviews and debates, I think it is fair to say that he charmed more often than he convinced his audience. He became adept at turning aside difficult questions with a joke or eirenic remark. When asked, as he often was, about the possibility of the Church ordaining women as priests, he would say, 'If we can, we should certainly do so. The question is: are we able to do so?'

Jack Kennedy, who had succeeded Cormac as Rector of the English College, became a close friend of his. The two of them went on many golfing holidays together, whether in Portugal or Ireland. When Cormac became Archbishop of Westminster in 2000, Jack, as a priest quite outside his jurisdiction, was very useful as a source of shrewd practical advice. Complaints were made that, during his time at Arundel and Brighton, Cormac had provided cover for a delinquent priest – complaints that he later admitted were justified. He refused to resign as archbishop, however, and instead took steps to put an end, once for all, to the scandal of paedophilia among the clergy. He set up a commission under Lord Nolan, of which he made Jack a member, and which produced a number of recommendations which he accepted. The wisdom of Cormac's proceedings soon became obvious to anyone who has followed the parallel between the English and the Irish Roman Catholic Churches. After the Nolan report, the English secular clergy have been comparatively free of scandals; in Ireland, the exposure of religious abuse of minors, and its ecclesiastical occlusion, reached such a pitch that the prime minister, Enda Kenny, broke off diplomatic relations with the Vatican.

Gordon Brown, when prime minister, invited Cormac to take a seat in the House of Lords. Because the Vatican disapproved of bishops taking part in politics, Cormac felt obliged to consult Rome before accepting. He waited a long time for a reply. When it came, he told me, it was in the following form: 'Forse si, e forse no: ma piuttosto no che si.'* That was sad: he would have made a genial contribution to the House's debates.

Cormac invited my wife and me to his installation as cardinal in Rome in 2001, and he and Jack were star guests at my eightieth birthday party in Balliol Hall in 2011. Sadly, in recent years, Cormac and I mainly got together to visit Jack's sickbed and to take part in his obsequies. At the beginning of 2017, Cormac himself paid a visit to death's door. Nancy and I lunched with him in his house in Chiswick after he left hospital and found him as warm and lively as we had known him to be for many years. Sadly, the respite was brief, and he died on 1 September 2017. Nancy and I were lucky to be able to visit him a few days beforehand, finding him once again alert and cheerful. My last words to him were the English College toast: 'Ad multos annos'.†

During this last visit, Cormac retold his story of recent papal conclaves. Of course, he never violated his vow to keep secret what happens within the meetings in the Sistine Chapel; but he was willing to talk about dinners with fellow cardinals before they entered the conclave. During the conclave that elected Pope

---

* 'Perhaps yes, perhaps no; but more no than yes.'
† 'May you live for many years.'

Benedict, he built up a group of anglophone colleagues that took an interest in the Jesuit cardinal from Latin America. Neither he nor I knew how influential this group was in the conclave of 2013, in which, as being over age, he took no part. But, as he told me at the time, after his election Pope Francis greeted him with the words: 'Tu sei colpevole.'*

---

* 'It's all your fault.'

# 3

# Three Anglicans

## Austin Farrer, Warden of Keble

Until I was in my twenties I had never met any Anglican clergy. In my Catholic youth I thought of them, collectively, as imitation priests. They were not very good imitations: their suits were not black enough and their clerical collars were too narrow. And, of course, Pope Leo XIII had determined in 1896 that 'ordinations enacted according to the Anglican rite have hitherto been and are invalid and entirely void.' Hence, Anglican ministers could not bring about the sacramental transformations which real – Catholic – priests could effect.

It was only while studying in Rome that I made any personal contact with Anglicans. One day in the English College I was told, 'The boss is giving a party for some Anglican bag.' Decoded, this meant that the rector was entertaining the Archbishop of York. 'Bag' was short for 'bagarozzo', an abusive Italian word for a priest: its polite meaning is 'black beetle', and children often hissed the word at us seminarians as we paraded the streets in our cassocks. Referring to the archbishop as a 'bag' might, I suppose, be taken as an initial step towards acknowledging the validity of Anglican orders.

Visits by Anglican prelates to the English College were, in those days, rare and chilly events, and it was not through Rome but through Oxford that I first became acquainted with a priest of the Church of England. A student who came to the seminary a year after me, Richard Incledon, was a graduate of Trinity College, Oxford. Something of a dandy, Richard stood out from the other seminarians because he always kept his black beaver hat polished to a resplendent sheen. He was a great source of gossip about Oxford, and especially Trinity, and it became clear to me that he was a great admirer of the then chaplain of Trinity, Austin Farrer, who was then in his late forties.

In the third year of philosophy at the Gregorian University, the student had to write a short dissertation as a condition of obtaining the licentiate degree. Influenced by Richard, I decided to choose as my dissertation topic a work of Farrer's on natural theology, *Finite and Infinite*, that had been published a decade earlier. It was unusual for a student to choose to research a work by a non-Catholic, and it may be that I needed some special permission to do so. I did, while in Rome, eventually secure permission to read books on the index, but I cannot now remember whether Farrer's book fell into one of the forbidden categories.

Whether forbidden or not, it was a formidable volume, and to this day I find it difficult to read. It developed a highly personal metaphysical system, and concluded with a 'Dialectic of Rational Theology', which listed and analysed 13 different proofs of the existence of God. Every such argument, Farrer argued, must proceed from a distinction within the finite world and show that the coexistence of the elements distinguished is intelligible only if God exists as the ground of such a coexistence.

The book ends with a striking paragraph:

> As I wrote this, the German armies were occupying Paris after a campaign prodigal of blood and human distress . . . Rational theology knows only that whether Paris stands or falls, whether men die or live, God is God, and so long as any spiritual creature survives, God is to be adored.

My copy is certified to have been produced 'in complete conformity with the authorized economy standards', and its crinkly paper and stark binding are a reminder of the difficulties of academic publishing during the war.

My dissertation was well received by the university authorities, and Incledon wrote to tell his old tutor about it. Farrer said that he was rather flattered to be the subject of a dissertation in a pontifical university, and invited me to Oxford to discuss his book with him. So during the summer of 1952, between the Roman philosophy and theology course, I visited him in Trinity, taking with me a list of questions, and we sat for several hours in the garden discussing finitude and infinity. It was my first experience of an Oxford tutorial, and my questions must have struck him as rather continental in style ('What, Dr Farrer, are the sources of your philosophy?').

I went to Oxford as a graduate student in 1957, just before Farrer published *Freedom of the Will*. I admired the book, but found it little help in writing my own doctoral thesis on the will, because of its unwillingness to engage with mainstream analytic philosophy. I believed that Farrer was intellectually quite the equal of Ryle, Austin and Ayer, but because of its idiosyncratic vocabulary and conceptual structure it failed to have the influence it deserved.

By the time I returned to Oxford as a layman, Farrer had become Warden of Keble. He welcomed me as a fellow don, and sympathized with my troubles with the Roman Catholic Church. Indeed, he was anxious to enrol me as a member of the Church of England, and offered to perform the appropriate ceremonies. Disappointed when I declined, he decided after a while that I was too much of an unbeliever to attend his philosophical discussion club, The Metaphysicals.

He remained friendly, however, and when he learned of my marriage he and his wife laid on a celebratory dinner in the lodgings at Keble. It was conducted in the old style grand manner, with the new wife sitting on the right of the host, and all the guests instructed not to depart until the bride and groom had taken their leave.

My last memory of Austin was of a quite different kind. In 1964, Denis Nineham was appointed to the Regius Chair of Divinity at Cambridge. To take up the post he needed a doctorate of divinity, and so he submitted his recently published Penguin commentary on St Mark's Gospel to be examined by the Oxford Faculty of Theology. Austin Farrer and Henry Chadwick were appointed examiners. Viva voce – oral – examinations in Oxford, though open to the public, rarely attract an audience, but on this occasion the lecture hall was full of senior and junior members anxious to watch a tournament between three of the senior theologians of the Church of England. Chadwick questioned Nineham in a gently urbane manner – but some of Farrer's questioning could only be described as savage. Though himself a venturesome interpreter of St Mark, he made it clear that he thought the commentary conceded too much to higher criticism of the Gospel. However, the examiners awarded the degree, and the occasion was remembered as the nearest thing to a medieval theological disputation to have occurred in the twentieth century. In 1968, Nineham succeeded to the wardenship of Keble on Farrer's untimely death.

## Henry Chadwick, Dean of Christ Church and Master of Peterhouse

In my early days as a don, I was much in awe of Henry Chadwick. He was nine years my senior, and his stature, his stately pace and his patrician voice made him a central figure in the ecclesiastical and academic establishment of Oxford. He was Regius Professor of Divinity, and had a formidable reputation as a patristic scholar, having produced a masterly edition of one of the most daunting texts of the Church fathers, Origen's *Contra Celsum*. In 1969, he became Dean of Christ Church, one of the most august posts in the diocese and the university.

When, in 1978, I became Master of Balliol, I was surprised to receive from Henry a warm and eloquent letter welcoming me into the fraternity of heads of house. I responded with enthusiasm, pointing out that the great Liddell and Scott dictionary of classical Greek showed that great things could be achieved if the heads of Christ Church and Balliol worked in collaboration with each other.

Henry and I did not in fact go on to collaborate in any great venture, and we were colleagues only for one year because he left to become Regius Professor at Cambridge in 1971. We did, however, share some philosophical and theological interests. A hero we had in common was the early Christian philosopher Boethius, the author of *The Consolations of Philosophy*. I had a special interest in Boethius' logic, and Henry in his music. When, in 1971, he published his splendid monograph on all aspects of Boethius, he went out of his way, at the launch party, to pay me undeserved compliments as a fellow researcher.

During the seventies and eighties, Henry was a leading member of the Anglican–Roman Catholic International Commission (ARCIC) that discussed the doctrinal issues separating the two communions. His wide historical learning, his negotiating skills, and his emollient manner made him a perfect member of the commission, and it was he who drafted crucial parts of the surprisingly conciliatory report on the Eucharist published in 1971. During this period he became friendly with my old friend, Cormac Murphy-O'Connor, who was one of his Catholic opposite numbers. He also played an important part in arranging for Pope John Paul II's visit to Britain in 1982. Later, he loved to show friends the stole that the pope had given him on that occasion. Given that the stole is the most sacerdotal of all vestments, it was hard not to see the gift as a tacit repeal of the condemnation of Leo XIII.

The work of ARCIC effectively came to a halt when the Church of England accepted the priesthood of women and the papacy remained unblinkingly opposed to any comparable step within its jurisdiction. Romans felt that the step showed that Anglicans placed fashion above ecumenism. Anglicans felt that Romans failed to adapt to the contemporary world. In particular, they found it hard to accept the argument, 'The first priests were the Apostles; the Apostles were all men; therefore only men can be priests.' I shared their scepticism: to me it seems no better than the argument, 'The first pope was St Peter; St Peter was married; therefore only a married man can be pope.'

In 1987, to the considerable surprise of his friends, Henry accepted the mastership of Peterhouse. The college was notorious for the degree of ill will among its fellows. The previous Master was Hugh Trevor-Roper, alias Lord Dacre. I had had dealings with Hugh over the production of *The History of the University of Oxford*, a project of which, for a time, I had oversight. Hugh was due to edit the volume concerned with the Tudor and Stuart periods, but years went by without any copy being delivered. Eventually, I was commissioned to deliver an ultimatum: if the next deadline was missed, his volume would be handed over to another editor. When I telephoned him with this message his response was, 'You have no idea how I am positioned. I am sure at Balliol you have some fellows who are bad, and some who are mad. But here at Peterhouse every single fellow is both bad and mad.'

Once again, Henry's gifts as a peacemaker were put to the test. But the most devastating event during his time at Peterhouse was not caused by the fellows. Henry was still in demand from time to time at the Vatican, and on one occasion he was asked to fly to Rome for a few days to offer advice. While he was away, the lift failed in the isolated Master's lodgings, and Peggy Chadwick was trapped inside it for 24 hours. She came out of the event psychologically unscathed, having exhibited the indomitable willpower for which she was famous among all who knew her.

Henry and Peggy had married in 1945, having been brought together by a common love of music. According to Rowan Williams' British Academy obituary of Henry, Peggy, a talented singer, liked to tell people that she had married her accompanist. But as an accompanist Henry was not at all monogamous. He used often to visit Rhodes House to accompany my wife singing Schubert lieder.

Henry took a benevolent interest in our younger son Charles, who read history at Peterhouse while he was Master. Charles founded a society called Peterhouse Left, but that did not prevent him from being on good terms with some ferociously right-wing tutors. One of the prized photographs in our study is of Henry, as acting Vice Chancellor of Cambridge, clasping Charles' hands as he conferred a BA on him.

## Richard Harries, former Bishop of Oxford

Like many nostalgic secular people, my wife and I commonly attend church on the great Christian feasts. For many years, we used to go to an Easter Sunday morning service in Oxford cathedral. There, one is offered the choice of attending matins, with a sermon by the

Dean of Christ Church, or Eucharist, with a sermon by the Bishop of Oxford. During the period when Richard Harries was bishop, and Eric Heaton was dean, the two preachers offered quite a different perspective on the feast of the resurrection. Harries would forthrightly state his belief in the narrative truth of the Gospel accounts, including that of the empty tomb. Heaton, on the other hand, delivered an ambiguous message, leaving one in doubt as to what he believed actually happened on the first Easter day.

Among the canons of Christ Church at that period were Oliver O'Donovan, an evangelical former Balliol student of mine, and Rowan Williams, the future Archbishop of Canterbury. After one particularly ambivalent sermon by the dean they looked at each other with puzzlement as they processed down the nave. Greek Christians are accustomed to greet each other during paschal time with the exchange, 'Christos aneste, Alethos aneste!' – 'Christ is risen, truly he is risen.' On this occasion, the two canons substituted, 'Christos aneste, Isos aneste!' – 'Christ is risen, *perhaps* he is risen.'

A few weeks after this Easter sermon, I found myself sitting at dinner next to Eric Heaton. 'Tell me Eric', I said. 'Do you really believe that the tomb was empty?' He turned to face me: 'What kind of person do you think I am?', he asked. It was a perfectly crafted response – well adapted to silence both questioners who would think him a fool if he answered yes, and those who would think him a knave if he answered no.

Over the years, Nancy and I became friends with Bishop Harries and his wife, and they were regularly invited to the January brunch with which we let in the New Year. The bishop would share star billing with the chancellor, and in my mind's eye I have a vivid picture of Richard and Roy, in our attic library, in vigorous argument about the pros and cons of Turkish membership of the EU.

Richard and I used to read each other's books, and occasionally review them. Though I was an agnostic and he a believer, our views on most ethical issues were very close to each other. I used to tease him by saying that he got them not from the Bible or the Church, but from the Enlightenment. In his most recent book, *The Beauty and the Horror*, he responds to this criticism by outlining lucid discussion of the competing claims that tradition and modernity make upon the religious believer. The merit of a tradition, he says, is that it gives us a distance from contemporary culture and a point of vantage from which to discriminate between genuinely new truths and mere passing fashions. Thus, the Anglican tradition has come to terms with new cultural norms – from biblical criticism in the nineteenth century, to female bishops in the twenty-first.

I find it hard to discover exactly what Richard believes about a personal afterlife and a general resurrection. But I find him, among my friends who are believers, the most rewarding person to discuss such issues with. It is now over 50 years since I left the Church, and while I am agnostic about the existence of God, I am not agnostic about life after death: I am sure that belief in it is an illusion. However, if – which God forbid – I should undergo a deathbed conversion, there is no Christian priest I would sooner have at my bedside than Richard Harries.

In the meantime, I am honoured to have been invited to join – as a part-time member, because of my age – an august group of walkers in the Chiltern Hills, of which Richard is the presiding spirit.

# 4

## Three Oxford dons

### Christopher Cox, fellow of New College

Christopher Cox went to Balliol in the early 1920s. Though he was a classicist, not a historian, he became, like many another Balliol scholar with a distinguished career ahead of him, a protégé of a history tutor, F. F. 'Sligger' Urquhart. Sligger invited him to join one of his reading parties in a chalet on a spur of Mont Blanc above Saint-Gervais. The chalet owed its existence to two eccentric beliefs of Sligger's father, David Urquhart, one time British Ambassador to the Sublime Porte. Urquhart senior believed that at a level of below five thousand feet the human mind did not function efficiently, being fuddled by an excess of oxygen. He also believed that the social problems of the nineteenth century would be solved if Turkish baths were built for Europe's poor: the rich would then no longer be able to despise them as the great unwashed. Accordingly, he built his summer retirement home in the Alps at around six thousand feet, and installed a Turkish bath.

Christopher never forgot his early visits to Sligger's chalet. In 1926, he became a fellow and tutor of New College, appointed to teach ancient Greek history. In 1946, however, he became a civil servant in the education department of the Colonial Office and its successors. He was the effective founder of a string of universities in colonies that were about to be given independence. Many of them gave him honorary degrees, but few of them thrived for long after release from colonial rule. After 1970, Christopher lived in retirement in New College, where he was given a suite of rooms, in spite of no longer being a member of the governing body. He served the college well, taking a keen interest in the welfare of the under-graduates and keeping open house on the model of Sligger.

When I first met him, Christopher was in his seventies. The alpine chalet was no longer open to Balliol reading parties, because Sir

Roger Mynors, to whom Sligger had left it in his will, had rather taken against the college when, in 1949, it failed to elect him Master. However, along with Tony Firth of University College, Christopher had, by the late 1960s, reinstated the tradition of Oxford reading parties at the chalet. Firth used to preside over University College parties for one half of the summer, and Cox over New College parties for the other half. At the suggestion of some of my Greats students, in 1970, I got permission from Mynors to make Balliol a third member of the consortium.

From then on, for 25 years, I visited the chalet, taking reading parties first from Balliol and then from Rhodes House. Once the initial pattern of three colleges' reading parties had been established, Mynors handed the chalet over to a charitable trust. Since the concept of a trust was foreign to French law it took all the skills of a leading QC – Jeremy Lever of All Souls – to devise the mechanism of ownership. The chalet became the property of a French société civile, whose two shareholders were two English companies whose sole function was to own the shares in the French company. The English companies in their turn were owned by the charitable trust, whose trustees thus only got their hands on the chalet through two pairs of metaphysical gloves. The first trustees were Christopher Cox, Tony Firth, Jeremy Lever and myself.

There were certain costs of being a fellow trustee with Christopher. He was excessively garrulous in person, and excessively copious on paper. He would appear, unannounced, perhaps in the middle of a tutorial, and announce, 'I have come to take your advice', after which there would follow 30 minutes of uninterrupted monologue. His handwriting was totally illegible, but just in case someone might be able to decode it he would finish a letter by scribbling over the already written text, like a Victorian correspondent anxious to get the maximum value out of the penny post.

Remaining sturdy into his seventies, Christopher never missed a summer visit to the chalet, even though it had no electricity, and running water came only from a nearby stream. To reach it, one had to take the rack-and-pinion Tramway de Mont Blanc, then walk for

40 minutes via the Hotel du Prarion, 20 minutes higher than the chalet, on which we depended for many of our supplies. Christopher was a beloved friend of the Hottegindres, the Savoyard family that had run the Prarion Hotel since the mid-nineteenth century. Mme Hottegindre once described Christopher's French to me as, 'Pas tout à fait correct, mais extremement riche.'*

Christopher insisted on having *The Times* brought up, six thousand feet, to the chalet every day. He said it was essential for him to read the obituaries. He used to draw on his extensive New College network in connection with the affairs of the chalet. If there was a local development that the Hottegindres wished to foster, or one that they wished to oppose, support would be lined up from alumni in the Foreign Office in London, or from current ambassadors in Paris. Letters would speed across the channel in diplomatic bags, eventually to baffle local mayors and officials in Haute-Savoie.

Unlike our Balliol reading parties, the New College parties under Christopher did their best to retain some of the formalities of the Sligger era. The Turkish bath was now a mere shower, but while Balliol parties brought sleeping bags, wore jeans and T-shirts, and did their own laundry, New College undergraduates slept between linen sheets and ate off white linen tablecloths which had to be carried down to the valley to be laundered.

Christopher, though a civil servant for much of his life, was one of the finest examples of a type of Oxford don that I fear is now almost extinct: a person whose whole happiness is bound up with the well-being – present and future – of the young undergraduates of the college to which they are proud to belong.

## Russell Meiggs, fellow of Balliol

Many people around the world knew Russell Meiggs better and longer than I did. I can speak at first hand only of the unique debt owed to Russell by the college which he served so energetically for

---

* 'Not exactly correct, but extremely rich.'

the greater part of his working life. At Balliol, I was his immediate colleague for six years: in the Greats course, he taught ancient history and I taught ancient philosophy. We shared a large number of classics students, and so I was privileged to watch, at close quarters, the devotion to his students which made him the most revered, and the most beloved, tutor of his generation.

Russell made friends of his students, and made them friends for life. He followed their careers, rejoiced in their successes, grieved over their misfortunes. They in turn kept him in mind wherever they were. When I would meet groups of Balliol alumni around the world, the first question they would ask about the college was, 'How is Russell Meiggs?'

He was the most effective tutor I have ever known. One thing he gave his students was an ability to see through what he called the Higher Nonsense. The other thing, most important, was that if you did want to find out about something – whether an immediate, practical matter, or an issue remote in space and time – you must throw yourself wholeheartedly into the quest for the truth.

He displayed this zest for discovery in his own work, whether on the Athenian empire or on timber in the ancient world – drawing on every kind of evidence, whether from literary texts, from inscriptions, or from physical remains lingering on the spot. All round the world others got drawn into the chase. Many a legend tells how Oxford colleagues on classical hillsides or in secular forests would meet a shepherd or a lumberjack who would say, 'If you are from Oxford you must know Meiggs.' Letters and postcards from the corners of the earth would bring scraps of evidence, and diplomatic bags would contain specimens relevant to his research.

Long before the younger generation of the sixties took to wearing their hair long, Russell was internationally well known for his enormous mane. He used to explain that he had to keep his hair long because there was only one barber in the world who could make a good job of cutting it, and he lived in Naples.

It was not only Russell's classics students who became and remained friends. Whenever he crossed the quad he would stop for a brisk word or a pointed joke with half a dozen students met at random. Whatever subject they were studying, the students could all recognize Mr Meiggs. For 25 years, Russell was in charge of Holywell Manor – a Balliol annex which was almost a college within a college. Running the manor brought Russell into contact with students from home and overseas, graduate and undergraduate, male and female, artists and scientists. It was not a classicist, but a young colleague in inorganic chemistry, who named his eldest son after him.

Russell was one of the shrewdest judges of character I have ever met. When we classicists shared students, he would notice at first meeting character traits which it would take the rest of us months to detect. However, Russell rarely expressed value judgements; and when he did, they were never malicious. I suppose the unkindest thing I ever heard him say about anyone was, 'That man has never looked a tree in the face in his life.'

What Russell did do was to make you judge yourself. He was so fearless in putting candid questions, and was himself so free of humbug, that conversation with him could be like a cold shower washing off one's own pretence and superficiality. In this respect, his Balliol colleagues owed him every bit as much as his students.

When Russell retired and went to Garsington, moving from Holywell to Pettewell, he entered fully into the life of the village, a member of the parochial church council, an eloquent speaker at parish meetings, a supporter of both football and cricket teams. He took the keen interest in the history of Garsington parish that he had taken in the history of the Athenian empire, and the first volume published by the Garsington History Society was dedicated to him. He was, I am told, as skilled at spotting future prodigies and future problems among the children in the primary school as among the candidates he used to interview for the Balliol classics course.

In later years, when his strength began to fail, a feature of the life of the village was sight of Russell's wheelchair being pushed up the hill by his wife Paula. Her inexhaustible energy won the admiration of all who had known her, whether at Balliol or in Garsington. Amid her family duties, and the cares of nursing Russell, by her books and editorial labours she won conspicuous academic distinction among historians of the seventeenth century. Such a combination of selfless personal devotion and scrupulous academic scholarship made manifest to all a fortitude of character comparable only to that of Russell himself.

Dr Samuel Johnson made a famous remark about Edmund Burke: 'If a man were to go by chance at the same time with Burke under a shed, to shun a shower, he would say, "this is an extraordinary man".' The same could be said with complete truth about Russell Meiggs: people who had met him only once remembered him for the rest of their lives.

If, in this, Russell was like Burke, in many other respects he reminded people of Dr Johnson himself. He had some of the same endearing eccentricities, and exhibited to his colleagues and students that hatred of self-deception which led Johnson to say to Boswell, 'My dear friend, clear your mind of cant.' Above all, he had the same ability to rise – by sheer power of will – above the recurrent threat of melancholy and the burden of disability and illness. Like Dr Johnson he retained, amid suffering, a deep and vivid religious faith, which was a wonder to others who had suffered less and who believed less.

## Richard Cobb, Professor of Modern History

Richard Cobb was one of the most celebrated historians of his generation, internationally recognized as an unrivalled authority on the French Revolution. When I first met him in 1964, he was a history tutor at Balliol, just one year senior to me. He had been brought to the college at the instigation of Christopher Hill, who admired his revolutionary writing and seems to have imagined him as a kindred left-wing spirit. Richard must have been a great disappointment to Christopher, because, as he once described himself, he soon became the most reactionary fellow of the college. His political views were eccentrically conservative, and his favourite students at Balliol were titled aristocrats such as Viscount Morpeth,

Lord Michael Pratt, and the future Sir David Gilmour. He also had a fascination with ceremonials and medals and crosses, and once lamented to me that, unlike the Légion d'Honneur, of which he was made a Chevalier in 1986, the British Academy did not give its fellows anything to wear.

Though Richard did not see eye to eye with Christopher, he was a firm friend of another of the history tutors, Maurice Keen. According to college legend, after a particularly convivial evening in the senior common room (SCR) the pair of tutors repaired to the door of the Master's lodgings and delivered a midnight serenade that awoke the Master, Sir David Lindsay Keir, a dour Ulsterman. In similar rowdy ventures, the pair were often joined by a third historian, Jack Gallagher, the Beit Professor of Commonwealth History. Jack was bitterly offended when, as a result of agitation by Marxist students, the governing body drew up a code of discipline that was to apply to senior as well as junior members.

The Balliol SCR was indeed sadly divided between 1968 and 1972 on how best to deal with revolutionary students of the era. Fellows on the Left supported the conciliatory tactics of the Master, Christopher Hill; fellows on the Right had more sympathy with the conservative dean, Frank McCarthy Willis-Bund. Frank was an Irish Protestant clergyman with an eighteenth-century horror of enthusiasm, whether in its religious or its political form. It was the dean's job to enforce discipline, and he had done so for years in a quiet and brisk fashion. But the Marxists in the junior common room (JCR) felt that he operated a double standard: public schoolboys' misbehaviour counted as juvenile high spirits, while the behaviour of those from state schools violated basic decencies. Under the new disciplinary code, the powers of the dean were much diluted, and a new disciplinary court was set up. Frank felt he had been betrayed, and his authority undermined by Christopher. Richard was very much on Frank's side. Years later, when I had succeeded Christopher, Richard told me that in those difficult days it was I who kept the college together, and that was why I was eventually chosen Master. I think what he meant was that I kept on good terms with both halves of the SCR. I did so on a simple principle, once described by Jasper Griffin as 'Voting with the Left and drinking with the Right.'

In 1973, Richard became Professor of Modern History, which meant that he had to give up his Balliol fellowship and move to Worcester College, to which the chair was attached. He frequently returned to dine in the college, especially when there was a feast. After attending a gaudy in 1979, he reported to a friend that he had enjoyed himself greatly: '*Le père Kenny*, unlike his predecessor Dr Hill, is not an enemy of pleasure and we all had a very good time.'

'Pleasure', for Richard, involved copious amounts of alcohol, and from time to time I was happy to join him in the pursuit of pleasure. While we were fellows together, he and I and one or two others would often stay on after dinner for an extra drink or two when most of the diners had left. It was not easy, however, to synchronize with Richard's potations because he had a habit of suddenly dropping off to sleep. I have known him sleep through a chancellor's speech at high table, waking up just in time to applaud energetically. After dinner, he might doze for a while, and then wake up full of thirst and energy just when the rest of us were thinking of going to bed.

It was one of Harold Macmillan's ploys – copied from Winston Churchill – when he wished to be rude to somebody, to pretend not to know who he was talking to. When Macmillan was chancellor, I watched him try this on Richard, who was sitting opposite him at a gaudy in 1981. Reminiscing about his experiences as a judge for the Wolfson Prize in 1979, he recalled that he had been made to read a dingy little book about the sewers and corpses of Paris, rather than the broad sweep of history. The book was Cobb's *Death in Paris*, and I was quite sure that the chancellor knew who he was talking to. But Richard, unfamiliar with the strategy, could only squirm in bafflement. He held his peace, he told his friends afterwards, because it was the diplomatic thing to do.

Even in the days when I saw a lot of Richard I knew that I was acquainted with less than half his life. He had a flat in Paris, and later a house in Normandy, and was even more famous in France than in England. He spoke French fluently, and his writing in French, I am told, is just as beautiful as the best of his English writing. Of all my Balliol colleagues, he was the most generous contributor to the gaiety of nations.

# 5

## Three heads of house

### Christopher Hill, Master of Balliol

When I was elected Master of Balliol, I joined a group of men and women who bore various titles – Master, Warden, Provost, President, Principal – but who had in common that they chaired the governing body of their college. (Woe betide those who thought they had more power than just that!) The collective description of such people is 'heads of house'. In the distant past, heads of house used to manage the entire university, meeting weekly as a Hebdomadal board. But after a series of reforms, the executive power had, by the twentieth century, passed to an elected body – Hebdomadal Council.

However, when in the nineteenth century heads of houses were stripped of most of their powers in university affairs, they clung on to one which then appeared of paramount importance: the choice of a lecturer to give an endowed series of sermons in the university church. In the 1980s, the only occasion on which they met collectively on university business was when they assembled as electors to the Bampton Lecturership. These meetings could be scenes of old world drama, as on the occasion when the noted liberal theologian Maurice Wiles was proposed as a candidate. Rachel Trickett, the colourful principal of St Hugh's, rose from her seat to say, 'May I point out that one of the duties of the lecturer is to refute heresy? How can Professor Wiles carry out that duty, being himself an heretic?' She proceeded to quote passages from his works to show that he was quite unsound on Chalcedonian doctrine. Wiles' tenure of the lecturership had to be delayed until a later election.

The first head of house that I met while a young clerical graduate student was Warden Sparrow of All Souls. I was introduced to him by the Canadian philosopher, Charles Taylor, then a fellow of that college. Lacking any knowledge of the Warden's tastes, I inquired, 'Is there a Mrs Sparrow?' His response was to grab my hand and to start massaging my palm with his thumb, leaving me in innocent bafflement.

In an Oxford life of 50 years, I must have met well over a hundred heads of house. The first I got to know well was my predecessor as Master of Balliol, Christopher Hill, the internationally known Marxist historian. One of my first duties as a young fellow of the college was to take part in his election to the mastership. The candidate I initially preferred, the former headmaster of Eton, 'Red Robert' Birley, was knocked out in an early round, and I switched my vote to Hill. Christopher, who had been a fellow of the college since 1938, was generally liked by the fellows, but some could not stomach his long membership of the Communist Party, which was terminated only in 1956 in response to Soviet repression in Hungary.

I once asked Christopher, after he had left the college, whether he had enjoyed being Master: 'It was wonderful to have been elected to it, and it is a wonderful post to have held . . .' he began – and then his voice tailed away. He was indeed Master at a difficult time, when many of the undergraduates enrolled in the revolutionary Left. During the student troubles of the late sixties and early seventies, he was caught in the middle. Right-wing dons would say, 'It is the likes of you, Christopher, that have put these silly ideas into the young men's heads.' The left-wing students, on the other hand, felt that Christopher was supposed to be on their side, and that he had sold out to the bourgeoisie.

At meetings of the conference of colleges, Christopher adopted a low profile. Many heads of house placed much of the blame for the troubles throughout the university at Balliol's door. Hugh Trevor-Roper's *Mercurius Oxoniensis* (the pseudo-seventeenth-century chronicler of Oxford's affairs) affected to believe that the Master of Balliol was no longer alive, having been hanged by the fanatics in his doctor's robes: 'The late Master was hustled to his grave at midnight, very obscurely . . . The Proctors have forgiven the young men who hanged their Master, as doubtless ignorant of the statutes against murther.'

Christopher was a firm believer in student participation in government, and several times tried to persuade us all that we should allow junior members on the executive committee which controlled the day-to-day affairs of the college. Most of us, who had listened to the time-wasting Marxist rhetoric in which the junior members indulged when the JCR met, from time to time, with the executive committee, regarded the proposal as a triumph of dogma over experience. But Christopher was persistent, and in 1976 he threatened to resign as Master unless the governing body voted junior members on to the executive committee. It took an emergency meeting of the fellows in Rhodes House to work out a compromise proposal and to persuade Christopher to withdraw his threat.

While Christopher's crusade for student government was not popular with many fellows, he carried almost all of us with him on another issue: he campaigned for years to the effect that the college should admit women as well as men. There would have been no difficulty in getting a majority of the governing body to vote to change our statutes, but that could be done only with the consent of the central university bodies. Since this was not forth-coming, Christopher arranged for the accommodation in the Balliol Annexe in Holywell Manor to be shared with St Anne's College. This joint graduate institution, set up in 1969, was the first mixed residential accommodation in Oxford. The Sex Discrimination Act 1975 weakened the power of the university to control the number of colleges who went mixed, and Balliol voted to do so in 1978. Sadly, it was only after Christopher had ceased to be Master that the change came into effect, but the decision was taken as a result of years of planning and persuasion on his part.

When I succeeded Christopher as Master, I did my best to move the college away from a position on the extreme Left to one closer to the Centre. This was popular with many older alumni: Anthony Powell published a diary in which he wrote: 'Kenny is obviously determined to put Balliol on the map again, after a dynasty of dreary Masters, either dull or actively harmful to the college.' But some of the changes I introduced were not at all popular with junior members. When we reintroduced formal hall dinners, abolished in the heyday of the revolutionary JCR, a masked figure appeared in the loft beneath the organ and shouted 'Long live the spirit of Christopher Hill.'

## Isaiah Berlin, President of Wolfson

During my years at Balliol, Isaiah Berlin was a regular visitor to the senior common room. Once a month, he would lunch with my colleague Alan Montefiore to discuss Jewish affairs. However, he and I were never very close, and I was only on the outer fringe of his vast international network of friends. Each of us had decided, after an initial foray into original philosophy, that we were more suited to be historians of ideas. But he knew next to nothing about the philosophers who most interested me, such as Aristotle and Aquinas, and I knew absolutely nothing about the post-Enlightenment philosophers that were his speciality. Both of us admired Wittgenstein, but Isaiah had no time for my Wittgensteinian friends. When one of them, Peter Geach, was proposed for a Cambridge professorship, Isaiah wrote to Bernard Williams, who held the other Cambridge chair: 'I do not myself believe in Geach's great intellectual gifts – only in a ferocious, narrow, path, which many schoolmen must have had whose memories have very rightly perished.' Of Isaiah's Zionist activities I knew nothing, even though he once invited to me lunch with Shimon Peres.

My first serious encounter with Isaiah was in 1984 when I wanted to arrange a commemoration of the fortieth anniversary of the death of Adam von Trott, a Balliol Rhodes Scholar who was executed in 1944 for plotting against Hitler. I had heard that Isaiah had been a friend of Adam's during their time at Oxford, and I asked his advice on organizing the event. I did not then know that during the war, Isaiah, in Washington, had been responsible for the negative attitude that allied leaders had taken to Trott's overtures on behalf of the Germans opposed to Hitler. Had I known, I would not have been surprised by Isaiah's unenthusiastic response to my proposal. However, he gave me the excellent advice to consult David Astor, the beginning of a lifelong and fruitful friendship for me. In answer to my inquiry, David drew up the cast list for a fine series of lectures on the German Resistance. The relationship between Adam and Isaiah was later the basis of Justin Cartwright's novel, *The Song Before it is Sung*, and Adam figures, thinly disguised, as one of the two protagonists of Robert Harris' recent novel, *Munich*.

Isaiah and I used to meet twice a year at meetings of the philosophy section of the British Academy. Whenever a name was proposed for election, Isaiah would reel off a potted biography of the candidate, laudatory or, more often, condemnatory. After some years, I became chair of the philosophy section, and one of my principal tasks was to prevent business being interrupted by vociferous gossip between Isaiah and Freddy Ayer at the back of the room.

It was impossible not to admire Isaiah's vast and vivacious erudition. But, like Samuel Johnson, he spoke better than he wrote. Moreover, his vocal gifts were more on display in conversation than in lectures, and his literary talent shone more in letters than in books. When Isaiah lectured it was as if streams of words bubbled up within him and mingled with each other to reach the outer world. Students would listen in admiration as wave followed wave of eloquence, but they would sometimes come away wondering whether the tide was going in or coming out – that is to say, for which side of a case Isaiah was arguing.

In later years, Isaiah and I became neighbours. I moved into a small house a few hundred yards from the grand Headington House in which Isaiah lived with his wife Aline. Isaiah was the unofficial squire of the village, and Aline was President of the Friends of Old Headington. The high perimeter of Headington House was, inevitably, known to the neighbours as the Berlin Wall.

From time to time, the Kennys and the Berlins exchanged hospitality. Once, turning up for a visit a little before the scheduled time, Isaiah pronounced, shaking his head, 'The worst form of unpunctuality is to arrive early.' Roy Jenkins, in the last years of his life, regularly celebrated New Year's Day by attending brunch in our house, and then going up the road to the Berlins for lunch. He was most downcast when one year this ritual was obstructed by some mishap to the Berlins' butler.

Isaiah would sometimes talk to me about music, and it was always fascinating to listen. But when his letters were published after his death they brought me some surprises. I had always assumed he was a keen admirer of Wagner, but I learned that he once wrote to Bernard Williams that he hated the atmosphere of Wagner's world: 'the Teutonic medievalism, the brutal relationships of the protagonists, the deeply neurotic relations of the men and women . . . that entire world is repellent to me'. He also said, improbably, that Wittgenstein had a policy of never speaking again to any person who professed in his presence an admiration for Wagner.

I was also astonished to learn that Isaiah could not read a score. How, I wondered, did he manage to build up such a powerful reputation as a music critic? Sure, one can acquire a refined taste merely by listening – but without being able to read notes on a page, how can one take in what is written by other critics when they quote passages? However, I brush aside any doubts about Isaiah's musical comprehension when I recall an occasion when, after my wife had given a recital of English and American songs in Holywell Music Room, he crossed the room to congratulate me on the beauty of her voice.

## Daphne Park, Principal of Somerville

A year after I became Master of Balliol, Daphne Park was elected as Principal of Somerville, the college where she had been an undergraduate during the war years. When she arrived in Oxford, her profession was officially described as 'diplomat', but an American friend in the CIA, who brought us together, made sure that I knew just a little of her spectacular career in the Secret Intelligence Service (SIS) that has recently been documented in Paddy Hayes' biography, *Queen of Spies*.

One of our first ventures together was to form part, with two other heads of house, of a deputation to the Secretary of State for Education to protest against recent policies of the Thatcher government, in particular the imposition of heavy fees on overseas students. Despite her links to members of the government, and despite the fact that she was in Oxford terms the junior member of the delegation, Daphne was the most forthright and vigorous in her protests.

If you travelled with Daphne, she would keep you entertained with stories of her adventures on delicate missions in Africa during the Congo wars. On one occasion, while driving through a deserted area she, had found her car surrounded by a threatening group of machete-armed militia. She jumped out of her car, and said, 'Oh, thank heavens you have come – I am having trouble with my carburettor.' She then opened the bonnet, twiddled some knobs while the men looked on, and then asked them to give her a push as she drove away. On another occasion, soldiers at Leopoldville airport, searching her baggage as she departed for Stanleyville, came on material which they took as indicating she was a supporter of Patrice Lumumba, whom the army had recently deposed. They decided to execute her.

'Why don't you let me go to Stanleyville?', she said. 'When I come back you can shoot me.'

'When are you coming back?'

'On Thursday.'

'OK', they said, as they let her on to the plane. 'But when you get back you will be shot.'

Fortunately, they seem to have forgotten to communicate the appropriate instructions to the posse that was on guard on the Thursday she returned.

Intrepid as she was in circumstances like those, Daphne did not find it easy to adapt to the cloistered surroundings of Somerville. The fellows complained that she did not understand how to deal with academics, and at the time of her arrival the academics were more than usually grumpy. Somerville had enjoyed the reputation of attracting all the cleverest women in Oxford. Now, since the men's colleges had begun to admit women, many of the brightest female candidates preferred to apply to Balliol or Corpus or Christ Church. This left the Somerville dons feeling that their college was being left with a much poorer field. Daphne believed that the college should follow the example of some other women's colleges and open its doors to men, but the governing body voted to remain single-sex. Later, the fellows altered their views, and in 1992 voted to amend its charter and statutes to admit men. But the undergraduates, and many of the alumnae, remained opposed to any change. An appeal was made to the Visitor, Lord Jenkins, who ruled in 1993 that the college had acted lawfully, but had failed to fulfil a moral obligation to consult the resident undergraduates. He imposed a gradual programme of transition which led to the ultimate acceptance of male students in 1994.

It might have been thought that the election of a Somerville graduate as the first female prime minister of the UK would have raised the spirits of the college. On the contrary, Margaret Thatcher was as unpopular in Somerville as she was elsewhere in the university. Many of the fellows turned out to vote down the proposal to give her an honorary degree. Daphne was mortified by what she saw as an act of gross discourtesy on the part of her colleagues. It also presented an obstacle to her efforts to repair the college's finances, since many of her wealthy contacts, who might be expected to make generous contributions, were keen admirers of Thatcher and affronted by the dons' hostility. None the less, Daphne persisted in her efforts, and by the time she retired as principal in 1989 she had raised the money to construct a new quadrangle and a new set of buildings – including a Margaret Thatcher Centre.

In the course of my life I have had three friends who were, or had been, spies. Each of them was a delightful companion, and I began to think that perhaps charm was an essential qualification for the profession. But then it occurred to me that maybe the most professional of the spies I have met were people whom I would never have dreamt had any connection with intelligence.

# 6

## Three benefactors

### Bill Coolidge, art collector

In the year 1926, Balliol College undertook a significant building programme, extending the junior common room and adding an extra storey to the main undergraduate building block. A major contribution to the cost of the enterprise was made by an anonymous benefactor. This turned out – though it was not public knowledge until much later – to be an American undergraduate then in residence – William A. Coolidge. Having taken his BA in 1927, Coolidge returned to the college as a member of the senior common room in 1933 to study law, in preparation for going to Harvard Law School. By the time I first met him, in 1978, he was 77 years old, and had been an honorary fellow of the college for 15 years.

His most remarkable benefaction to the college was the setting up of the Atlantic Crossing Trust, familiarly known as the Pathfinder Scheme. This provided a travel grant and pocket money for eight Balliol finalists to travel to America and enjoy the hospitality of a network of hosts that Bill had built up among his friends and returning American Balliol alumni. Having travelled across the Atlantic by liner at Bill's expense, the fortunate Pathfinders would be welcomed to his house, introduced to his excellent clarets, and issued with a Hertz credit card and a list of addresses. Many of the most distinguished Balliol graduates of the post-war years – such as Peter Brooke, Chris Patten and Edward Mortimer – benefited from the Pathfinder Scheme, and have been grateful during their careers for the contacts made during their US visit. Not all Pathfinders, however, showed appropriate gratitude. Particularly during the JCR's Marxist years there were those who would make it a point of honour during their tour to denounce American capitalism to their American capitalist hosts.

Bill lived in a handsome house in Topsfield, Massachusetts. With wealth inherited and enhanced, he had built up an exceptional collection of paintings. Guests dined beneath a Rubens and an El Greco, and woke in the morning to admire a Turner at the head of the bed and a Renoir at the foot. Bill would show guests lovingly round his main picture gallery. But when I knew him, his sight had begun to fail, and it was heart-rending to see him point out features on canvases that he could no longer see, but that were graven on his memory. I once tried to persuade him to bequeath to Balliol his El Greco of Saint Catherine, the college's patron saint; but Bill did not want to break up his collection, and the painting is now in the Museum of Fine Arts, Boston.

In 1982, a problem arose in connection with the Pathfinder Scheme in that, for the first time, there were women as well as men among the Balliol finalists who were the normal candidates for Pathfinder awards. My wife and I travelled to Topsfield to persuade Bill to accept this development, but his response was so full of alarm that for the year 1982 it was decided not to send any female Pathfinders. Instead, the women who had been elected were given travel grants by the college from its own funds, and arrangements for hospitality of the kind that Bill made for male Pathfinders were made for the women by my wife's parents, Mr and Mrs Henry T. Gayley of Ithaca, New York.

A year later, Bill accepted that there would be women Pathfinders, and henceforth they were elected by the college annually in the normal way. However, for some time he found it difficult to welcome this development, especially as his health was deteriorating. He used to tell me that he could no longer take pleasure in meeting with Pathfinders in the way he had in the past. But by 1988 he had become reconciled to the visits of female Pathfinders, and indeed had taken such a liking to one of them as to make her a gift of silver plate.

Throughout his life, Bill continued his generosity to Balliol: he was a major contributor to the centenary appeal of 1963 and the Dervorguilla Appeal of 1983. Guests who dine in the college today greatly admire the silver candlesticks he presented to high table, once the property of Stanisłas II of Poland. Shortly before his death, he devised a new plan for academic exchanges of faculty between Balliol and MIT, and after his death his heirs made arrangement for the Pathfinder Scheme to continue. Few benefactors over the centuries have so well deserved a permanent place in the college's bidding prayer.

## Irwin Miller, businessman and philanthropist

Nowadays, every head of an Oxford college is expected to devote time and effort to fundraising. I was fortunate to have been elected to such a post before it was an essential part of the job. However, Balliol did ask me to raise two million pounds in celebration of the septcentenary of the college receiving its first statutes in 1273 from the Lady Dervorguilla. She was the widow of John de Balliol, and proved herself a more generous benefactor than her parsimonious husband. The college had, in fact, already had a septcentenary appeal in 1963, but we hoped people had by now forgotten about that – and, in any case, our historians now assured us that the foundation date of 1263 was dubious. Two million pounds would be laughed at today as the target of an appeal, but to me in those days it seemed a massive sum to raise.

Before launching the appeal, I set off on a tour of Balliol millionaires to ensure advance pledges. In my career as a beggar I have met no benefactor more agreeable than J. Irwin Miller, who was one of my first ports of call. Irwin had come to Balliol from Yale in 1931, and had rowed in Torpids and Eights and at Henley, while taking a second-class degree in PPE. He had gone on to a gallant war career in the US Navy, taking part, on the fleet carrier *USS Langley*, in the invasion of the Marshall Islands. For most of his life thereafter he had been President of the Cummins Engine Company of Columbus, Indiana.

Irwin's relationship to Columbus was very similar to that of the early Medici to Florence. Columbus was the company town of

Cummins Engine in the same way as the Medici bank was the main enterprise of Florence. Like Cosimo and Lorenzo, Miller held no public office, but effectively ran the city in informal ways. Most of all, he resembled them in bringing beauty to his home city. This he achieved by a remarkable offer to the city fathers: he promised that he would pay the architect's fees for every public building, provided that the architect was chosen and the design approved by a special panel of his choice, headed by Eliel Saarinen.

In this way, the town of Columbus became an exhibition of the finest specimens of twentieth-century architecture. Saarinen himself designed the first of the buildings erected under the scheme – the First Christian Church on Fifth Street – as well as a building for the company's bank, the Irwin Union Bank and Trust Company. Architects chosen by Saarinen went on to design the elementary school, the ice arena, the salvation army corps, the adult education centre, the fire station and a host of other buildings, including several more schools. The town long ago became a tourist attraction, and Martin Randall Travel now advertises a tour of Galleries of the American Midwest, of which a prime attraction is a private visit to Irwin's own house – 'a perfect example of a complete modernist house'. Most recently, the film *Columbus* celebrates the uniqueness of the town.

Irwin was the easiest possible person to ask for a favour. If I went to spend the weekend with him and his wife Xenia he would say, early on the Friday evening, 'Tony, I am sure there is something you would like me to do for the college. Tell me what it is, and I'll tell you whether I can do it or not. Then we can enjoy the weekend together.' And enjoy it we did, touring the town's architectural splendours one by one.

Irwin was a devout, but liberal, Christian. On my first visit, he was due to preach on the Sunday morning in the North Christian Church, one of the town's magnificent ecclesiastical buildings. He asked me to help him identify a passage in Eusebius' *Ecclesiastical History* which he wanted to use against fundamentalists in the community. He was also involved in interfaith dialogue, and was proud to have been awarded the Order of St Vladimir by the Russian Orthodox Church.

In 1981, Miller came into the public eye as a member of President Carter's Eminent Persons Group – officially known as the Study Commission on US Policy Toward Southern Africa. As a result of this, he and I were drawn together in a quite different context, as I will explain later in this chapter.

## David Astor, journalist and philanthropist

David Astor came to Balliol in 1934, the same year as Irwin Miller, but he was unhappy in the college and left without a degree. I did not know him in the great years between 1948 and 1965 in which he was editor of *The Observer*, but I have known people who worked for him at that time and who worshipped him thereafter. As mentioned in an earlier chapter, I first met him in connection with the lecture series in memory of Adam von Trott, but it was in connection with the affairs of Ireland that I became close to him.

Early in the 1980s, I was asked by Lord Longford to write, for his firm Sidgwick & Jackson, a memoir of my Catholic days. The editor who took care of my book was Marigold Johnson, and it was given the name *A Path from Rome* by her husband Paul. Marigold introduced me to an organization called the British-Irish Association (BIA), a charity devoted to political education. It used to bring together on neutral ground, commonly in Oxford or Cambridge, representatives of different factions in the troubled province of Northern Ireland, and politicians and civil servants from the British and Irish governments. One of its founders, and its then chair, was none other than David Astor. He quickly, with Marigold's help, drew me into the affairs of the group.

More than once I offered Balliol as a venue for meetings of the association. Not all the fellows were happy with this: they were uneasy when sniffer dogs explored the college in preparation for the conferences, and potential IRA targets, such as the chief constable of the RUC, slept in college bedrooms. But the meetings were valuable adjuncts to the peace process. Northern Ireland politicians of different persuasions, who would hesitate to be seen together on home ground, would fraternize happily in the JCR bar in the small hours. It was even possible to hold interdenominational services on the Sundays of the conferences, though in the early days they did not seem to consist of much more than the Lord's Prayer and a minute's silence.

One of the Balliol meetings of the British-Irish Association was scheduled for September 1985. A week before it was due, David, Marigold and I were summoned to the Cabinet Office. The Cabinet Secretary, Robert Armstrong, asked us to postpone the meeting. Discussions between the British and Irish governments were well on the way to reaching an agreement, we were told, but informal public discussions of the kind that took place at BIA meetings might prove disruptive at a critical point.

We agreed to the postponement, but none the less the police insisted on a thorough search of the college because the IRA had a habit of concealing bombs weeks before they were primed to explode. The police crawled over the buildings, taking up floorboards here and destroying suspicious objects there. The climax came when a sniffer dog began to bark in the middle of the fifteenth-century library. This was supposed to indicate the presence of gunpowder, but a controlled explosion would have risked destroying the college's collection of rare books. 'Is there any appeal against the dog's decision?', I asked. It was agreed to send for one of the Queen's dogs from Windsor Castle to give a second opinion. The superior dog trotted through the library, nose in air, without emitting a sound. The junior sniffer, to my great relief, was overruled.

Two months later, the Anglo-Irish Agreement was signed by the prime minister and the Taoiseach in Hillsborough Castle. For the first time, the British government allowed the government of the Republic a formal role in the administration of Northern Ireland. David and I were pleased that the informal meetings we had arranged had helped to facilitate this important forward step in the peace process in the province. Some years later, I succeeded David as the chair of the British-Irish Association, but by that time he had involved me in another of his benevolent conspiracies.

David had long been active in South African affairs. While editor of *The Observer*, he had sent parcels of books to the imprisoned Nelson Mandela, warning that if the books were prevented from reaching their destination he would make it front-page news. In 1985, he began to worry about the condition of post-apartheid South Africa. If the African National Congress (ANC) came to power, would it have enough members with the experience needed to run the country? Or would the new South Africa be like Angola after the Portuguese withdrawal, with the new rulers lacking basic competences?

At the suggestion of Ann Yates, a South African friend living in Oxford, David and I and some others started an organization to help train exiled members of the ANC for the kind of job they would have to do once apartheid ended. We discovered that the ANC was not short of educationally qualified members – there were 2,000 PhDs in exile in Lusaka. The difficulty was what Oliver Tambo called 'the parking problem' – an opportunity for these exiles to exercise their skills in an appropriate professional capacity. In 1986, we founded the Southern African Advanced Education Project (SAAEP) 'to provide practical training and experience for black South Africans and to prepare people against the day when they would be needed for key roles in a new South Africa'.

Naturally, we needed the approval of the ANC for our activities, and David had had initial discussions with Oliver Tambo, the head of the movement. But when the time came for the trust deed to be signed, Tambo was in hospital. Nelson Mandela was still in prison, and we did not trust Winnie Mandela. So I invited Adelaide Tambo to Balliol to give her blessing to the project. She was a traditionally built lady with a regal presence, and when I brought her into the senior common room a great hush fell upon the chattering fellows at their buffet lunch. She listened to our plans and approved them. But as she was leaving she said to me, 'Are you not worried about working with the ANC? You know Mrs Thatcher doesn't like us much, and you might lose your job.' I responded that for that matter I did not like Mrs Thatcher much, but that fortunately she did not have the power to fire me.

The activities of the trust were organized very efficiently by Ann Yates, and SAAEP fellows were found placements with local authorities, national utilities, sports organizations, newspapers and broadcasting stations. The Overseas Development Administration, under Chris Patten, was sympathetic to our efforts once it learned what we were doing. Private industry was at first rather suspicious, but Irwin Miller, fresh from his experience with the Eminent Persons Group, led the way by offering ANC members placements with the Cummins Engine Company. By the time the trust was wound up in 1995, 700 individuals had benefited from tailor-made training and work courses of between three months and two years.

When I moved to Rhodes House, I did not have the same opportunities to work with David, but kept meeting people who were involved in projects that he was unobtrusively sponsoring – a chair of archaeology here, a shelter for battered wives there, and so on. He was instinctively ready to take on causes that were unpopular, such as the welfare of the Moors Murderer Myra Hindley. He told me that he believed that Lord Longford's vociferous campaign on her behalf was counterproductive. He had told him, 'Frank, if you'll shut up, I'll take care of Myra.'

Towards the end of my time at the Rhodes Trust, my work did bring the two of us together again. I was writing a centenary history of the trust, and an important figure in that history was one of my predecessors as secretary, Philip Kerr, later Lord Lothian. Lothian had been in love with Nancy Astor, David's mother, and had been converted by her to Christian Science. Some people used to believe that Lothian was in fact David's father. I do not know whether any still do, but for my part I am sure that the love between Philip and Nancy remained Platonic: they were both, in different ways, too puritan to let it go further.

In order to find out more about Lothian for my book, I had conversations with David about his childhood. The two of us had in common that we had each abandoned the faith of our highly religious mothers. David was reluctant to talk about his religious differences with his mother, but was willing to talk about the importance of Lothian in his life: 'He meant much to me', he said. 'More than my own father.'

# 7

## Three businessmen

### Warwick Fairfax, newspaper magnate

Sir Warwick Fairfax came from a distinguished Sydney dynasty. His father, Sir James O. Fairfax, and two of his uncles, had been under-graduates at Balliol in the days of Benjamin Jowett. He himself came up from Sydney University in 1921 to read Philosophy, Politics and Economics (PPE). He became managing director and then chair of the family firm, John Fairfax and Sons, who were publishers of *The Sydney Morning Herald*. By the time I got to know him, in the 1970s, the firm appeared to own pretty well all the Australian newspapers that were not owned by Rupert Murdoch, in addition to a number of television stations.

Sir Warwick was interested in philosophy, a subject in which he deemed himself an expert. He decided to endow a fellowship in the subject in his old college, and a few years after arriving at Balliol I became the first Fairfax Fellow. The duties of the fellowship included taking long walks round and round the quad with Sir Warwick during his visits to Britain, listening to his philosophical discourses and interjecting the occasional 'Up to a point, Sir Warwick.'

Instead of giving the college a sum of money to invest as an endowment for the fellowship, Sir Warwick handed over a quantity of shares in John Fairfax and Sons Ltd. Like an earlier Oxford benefactor, Cecil Rhodes, he seems to have believed that fellows of colleges were 'as children in the affairs of the world', and could not be trusted to make wise investments.

Sir Warwick had two sons by two different wives. The son by the first wife, James, came to Balliol in 1952: he became a gifted art collector. The son by the second wife, Warwick junior, arrived as a student shortly after I became Master. His parents came to stay with my wife and myself in order to supervise young Wocka's entry to the college. Lady Fairfax disapproved of the décor of his rooms, and complained loudly to the bursar. It was the worst possible start to a young man's college life.

While I was touring the world in quest of funds for the Dervorguilla Appeal, I included a trip to Australia to beg from alumni there. The Fairfaxes entertained me handsomely in their country house: beside my bed was a handle which enabled the roof to be rolled back so that one could sleep under the stars. However, I quite failed to persuade Sir Warwick to endow a second fellowship. Indeed, I left Australia without having collected a penny for the college. To cover my travel expenses I gave a number of philosophy lectures in various universities.

After Sir Warwick died, young Warwick tried to wrest control of *The Sydney Morning Herald* from his half-brother James. Warwick was poorly advised, and made an excessively high bid. In order to pay back what he had borrowed from the banks, he had to sell off the other assets of the family company. The gainers, of course, were the previous shareholders, who were paid over the odds. This group included both James Fairfax and Balliol. The Balliol shares had trebled in value since they were acquired, and the proceeds enabled a second Fairfax Fellowship to be set up. James contributed generously to the college's building plans, and there is now in Holywell Manor an elegant quadrangle bearing his name. Meanwhile, poor Warwick was mocked in the newspapers as 'Wocka the Terminator'.

## Robert Maxwell, publisher

In the early 1960s, Robert Maxwell expressed the wish to create a fellowship at Balliol. If I remember rightly, he wanted some academic work to be done about the best way to curb the power of trades unions. There was solemn debate about whether to accept the offer, particularly among the science fellows. The older among them did not want to have anything to do with the owner of Pergamon Press, because its journals published scientific rubbish. The younger ones, however, said that the scientific establishment was so stuffy that Pergamon provided the only way for bright new ideas to get published. Youth won the debate, and so there began a long and often close connection between the college and the Maxwell family. Three of Robert's sons came to Balliol – Philip in 1966, Ian in 1975, and Kevin in 1982.

My own first contact with Robert Maxwell was unconnected with the college. In 1978, I published a book, *The Aristotelian Ethics*, that was an early venture in stylometry – that is to say, the statistical study of style. When I wrote it, there were many textbooks of statistics for students of science and medicine, but there was nothing in English for the historian or the literary scholar. When I finished my work on Aristotle I decided to write the textbook I wished I had had while I was working on the text. In it, I took all the examples and exercises from literary contexts, and moved at a gentle pace suitable for those with no more than A-level mathematics. Thinking that a conventional publisher might be unwilling to take on such an oddly conceived book, I offered it to Pergamon. Maxwell gave it a warm welcome, but turned down the various titles I suggested. He insisted that it be called *The Computation of Style*, though the techniques it explained required no more than a pocket calculator. The book would only sell, he told me, if the title contained some allusion to computers.

It turned out that one reason Maxwell was interested in stylometry was that his wife, Betty, was doing a doctoral thesis concerned with some correspondence of her nineteenth-century French ancestors, and wished herself to use a computer to make some statistical analyses. There were few people in the modern languages department at that time willing to assist her, and so I was appointed an additional part-time supervisor of her dissertation. When the thesis was approved for the doctorate, Robert gave a grand party in his house of Headington Hill Hall. Betty was a delightful person to work with, and it was good to see the pride that her husband took in her.

In 1981, Maxwell's daughter Ghislaine applied to come to Balliol to read modern languages. Given that she had a French mother, I expected there would be no problem about her competence; but no – the French tutors decided that her A-level results were not up to the mark. It fell to me to telephone the news to her father: 'Bob', I said nervously, 'I have some bad news for you. We aren't going to take Ghislaine.' I waited for the thunderbolt to fall: 'Quite right!', came the answer, 'She's an idle chit of a girl. I'll make her do some serious work and send her back to you next year.' And indeed, when she returned the following year she had improved her grades and was accepted.

Ghislaine had a successful undergraduate career, but not without problems. In her second year she received a kidnapping threat, which had to be taken seriously after a grandson of J. Paul Getty had been kidnapped and had his ear cut off. The dean of the college placed her under discreet surveillance.

Two years later, my wife and I were invited to a lavish birthday party in Headington Hill Hall in honour of Maxwell's sixtieth birthday. Asparagus, lobster, *boeuf* Wellington and grapefruit mousse were followed by a string of eight speeches from distinguished guests. Several of the speakers were ambassadors from the communist East who were attending in honour of Pergamon's publishing exploits behind the Iron Curtain. A speech from Harold Wilson stood out for its wit and brevity. Each speech was followed by a response from the birthday boy. Thanking the Bulgarian ambassador for awarding him an honorary degree, Maxwell said: 'In the heart of every English man and woman there beats a note of friendship for Bulgaria.' This was too much for a lady at our table who said audibly, 'Not in mine there doesn't.' She slipped off her chair, and had to be escorted away by her husband.

At the time of the Dervorguilla Appeal, I found Maxwell extremely helpful. This was surprising because the chief fundraiser of the appeal was Rodney Leach, who had only a year or two earlier headed an inquiry that found Maxwell not to be a fit and proper person to run a company. The two of us visited him and asked him for a contribution to a particular building that was to cost £500,000. Maxwell persuaded a Japanese friend to contribute £200,000, and Rodney

Leach persuaded the financier Jack Dellal to offer £200,000. I found another £50,000, and then got back to Maxwell: would he take us over the top? He agreed to do so – but there was a snag: Dellal had made his gift conditional on the building being named after him. Maxwell made no difficulty at all about this, in spite of having been the major facilitator for the building. After his death, when his name was in bad odour, the college was glad that it had a Dellal building rather than a Maxwell building.

Occasionally I was invited, with one or another head of house, to lunch at Headington Hill Hall in order to strengthen the management team in negotiations with employees of Mirror Newspapers. These were bizarre occasions, and I never felt that the burly Scottish trades unionists that we lunched beside were in any way impressed by the presence of a few effete Oxford dons. On the other side, Maxwell felt that he had been let down by the college because the projected academic plan for the defeat of the trades unions never saw the light of day.

In 1985, I again approached Maxwell as a publisher. When the Anglo-Irish Agreement was reached, I wanted to write a book explaining its terms and the events that led up to it. I had several discussions with Maxwell about the form it should take. What he wanted was for me to write a short book, to be distributed free with copies of the *Daily Mirror*, calling for a British withdrawal from the six counties and a united Ireland. When I told him I could not possibly do that, he agreed to publish the book all the same, and it appeared in 1986 as *The Road to Hillsborough*.

In 1991, Maxwell was found dead after falling overboard in the Canaries from his motor yacht, the *Lady Ghislaine*. To this day, it has not been settled whether his death was accident, suicide or murder. Recently, Balliol put up a handsome list of its benefactors carved in stone. The name of Maxwell is not among them, even though he brought more money to the college than many of those named. To me this seems disgraceful. It would, of course, be a different matter if the college had decided to repay an equivalent sum to the pension funds that Maxwell gutted in his desperate last days.

# John Templeton, philanthropist

In 1983, there was a celebration at Rhodes House to mark the eightieth anniversary of the Rhodes Trust. The Queen and the Duke of Edinburgh were the guests of honour. I was commissioned to present to Prince Philip a 1934 Rhodes Scholar, John Templeton, a world champion investor who had made many millions by buying up penny shares. I explained to the Prince that Templeton had just made a gift of £3 million to convert the Oxford Centre for Management Studies into Templeton College. The Prince did not forget that he was Chancellor of Cambridge University. He tempered his congratulations with the remark, 'I can think of another place where the money could have been better spent.' Having had my own eye on Templeton as a potential benefactor to his old college of Balliol, I could only murmur to myself 'That makes two of us.'

Later I was placed on the advisory board of Templeton College. The benefaction was not a large one to establish an entire college, and I once asked John why he had not offered a more generous endowment: 'It's a school for business studies', he said. 'It's not going to be any good unless it teaches people how to raise money for themselves.'

He made me a trustee of the college's endowment, and we used to meet a couple of times a year to discuss its investment. Some of John's proposals were hair-raising. In one year, he proposed that we sell all our holdings and place half the proceeds in New Zealand bonds and the other half with an investment manager in Hong Kong who, I happened to know, placed his trades on the basis of astrology. It was difficult for me to challenge the judgement of one of the world's most successful investors, but fortunately a fellow trustee – a hard-headed oil magnate – was able to convince John that such a portfolio would not be well viewed by the Charity Commission. As time went on, the endowment proved more and more inadequate, and the college was forced into amalgamation with another institution to make what is now Green Templeton College.

Other than investment, John's greatest concern was with religion. In 1970, he founded the Templeton Prize for progress in religion and set it at a value comparable to that of the Nobel Prizes. Since then, many distinguished people have been awarded the prize, though it has changed its original name. John once asked me to serve on the panel of judges who select the prizewinners. I refused, on the grounds that in religion there was no objective test of progress: 'Tell me, John', I said, 'was Martin Luther a disaster for religion or a great leap forward?' He later temporarily offered the prize for progress in human values.

Once the prize had become well known, John persuaded Prince Philip to present it to each year's winner. On the one occasion I attended the ceremony in Buckingham Palace – I was there because I had been chosen to make the speech commending the winner – the prince appeared to have forgotten the occasion and had to be brought in from some gardening work.

In 1981, John published a book entitled, *The Humble Approach*. He was one of two people I have known who published books on humility. The other was Lord Longford. Neither of the two authors was a conspicuous exhibit of the virtue whose merits they extolled.

John was keenly interested in the relation between science and religion, and his major foundation was devoted to bringing the two together. He set up a menu for specific researches, some of which were rather bizarre. The most famous venture of the foundation was the Great Prayer Experiment of 2006 – an empirical test of the proposition that praying for sick patients improves their health. Three churches in different parts of America mounted prayer campaigns, and 1,802 coronary bypass patients were divided into three groups: (1) those who were prayed for, but did not know it; (2) those who were not prayed for, and did not know it; (3) those who were prayed for and were told so. When the results were published, there was no difference between those who were prayed for and those who were not; oddly, those in group (3) fared worse than those in group (1). The experiment was widely mocked, but it was very much in the spirit of John Templeton.

The foundation has indeed also produced useful work, particularly in the years when its chief executive was Chuck Harper. He focused its research on issues in which scientists and theologians did have important things to say to each other. I attended an excellent conference in Paris on the origin of the world. There, first-rate cosmologists and ranking theologians found it possible to engage in constructive dialogue. But after John died, his son, Dr Jack Templeton, under the slogan 'Let Sir John be Sir John', let Harper go, and threw away the academic respectability that he had acquired for the foundation.

To me it seemed as if John's son wished to turn the foundation into the basis of a personality cult. I was a member of the foundation's advisory board at the time, and decided to resign in protest. It turned out that I had no need to do so since my term of office was due to run out, and Dr Jack had no intention of renewing my tenure. Now that Dr Jack is himself dead, it remains to be seen in what direction the foundation will travel.

# 8

# Three Oxford philosophers

## Gilbert Ryle, Waynflete Professor of Metaphysics

In my first year as a student at the English College in Rome, I was given by a tutor a copy of a recently published work by an Oxford philosopher, Gilbert Ryle. In *The Concept of Mind*, Ryle conducted a sustained attack on Descartes' account of human nature, which he mocked as the doctrine of 'the ghost in the machine'. The book, full of concrete examples and witty sallies, gripped my imagination and introduced me to a style of philosophy very different from the desiccated neo-scholasticism of the Gregorian University.

Ryle's criticism of Cartesianism bore some resemblance to Wittgenstein's later philosophy, and to this day it remains uncertain how far in his book he was drawing on Wittgenstein's thought, and how far he had independently reached similar conclusions. When Ryle's book appeared, *Philosophical Investigations* had not yet been published, and Wittgenstein's ideas were circulating only in samizdat. Elizabeth Anscombe once told me that, while reading the *The Concept of Mind* shortly after it appeared, she went to meet Wittgenstein off a train, and felt obliged to conceal the book under a wrapper. This did not prevent the great man from snorting with disapproval when he discovered what she was reading.

I first met Ryle myself when I attended his seminars as a graduate student in the late 1950s. His lecturing manner was bluff and down to earth, and his responses to questions could take the form of a brisk bark. But he was a genial person, always kind to students, however rude he might be about his colleagues. In my student days, he and J. L. Austin were the leading members of the philosophy sub-faculty. Austin was the better lecturer, and I enjoyed the gusto with which, lecturing under the title 'Sense and Sensibilia', he attacked the positivism of A. J. Ayer. He would read, with evident distaste, the opening paragraph of some recent work of Ayer's, and then say, 'So there you see displayed what we may call the bottom of the garden path.'

Whereas Ryle encouraged young students, Austin could enjoy setting traps for them and watching them fall in. During one of his instruction sessions he made some disparaging remarks about Aristotle. 'Who, then, do you regard as the best ancient philosopher?' I asked. 'Cratylus', was the reply. I queried innocently, 'And which of his works do you recommend us to read?' 'As you know', he snarled back, 'Cratylus left no writing but philosophized only by moving his finger.'

With a Hungarian graduate student, Julius Kovesi, I produced a cyclostyled periodical called *WHY?*, which contained a number of philosophical spoofs and parodies. The first issues that appeared, in 1958, attracted a certain amount of attention, not all of it friendly. One day after his class, Austin said to me: 'I see you and Kovesi have taken to bringing out a comic. I am sorry to see him involved in this – *he* has real philosophical talent and might be spending his time more profitably.'

I had personal experience of Ryle's generosity when I left the priesthood and was looking for a job as a philosopher. I wrote to ask if he knew of any vacancies. 'More likely than unlikely that we'll find you a berth before the end of the academic year', he wrote back, accompanying his reply with a tactful offer to help financially if I was short of funds. He passed word around Oxford that I was available, and on his recommendation Balliol encouraged me to apply for a fellowship there.

After I had been elected to the fellowship, I wrote to him on some point of business, addressing him as 'Dear Professor Ryle'. He wrote back, 'Dear Kenny', and insisted that I must address him as 'Dear Ryle' – 'We are colleagues now, I am glad to say.' I did not ever dare to propose that we should use each other's Christian names.

By this time Austin had died, and Ayer had taken up a professorship in Oxford. Though very widely known for his pre-war book, *Language, Truth and Logic*, Ayer was felt by many in Oxford to be yesterday's man. Ryle was now the undoubted doyen of Oxford philosophy. This was still in its self-confident heyday: linguistic philosophy was in its 'ordinary language' phase, and Oxford came to be regarded as the centre of this movement. The philosophy department contained more philosophers than any other in the world, and from all over the English-speaking world philosophers gathered to sit at their feet, and even at the feet of Oxford figures then holding junior posts.

Ryle's influence was exercised partly through his editorship of *Mind*, then the most prestigious philosophical journal. His editorial methods were rough and ready. 'Is it true, Professor Ryle', one American visitor asked, 'that you accept or reject an article on the basis of reading just the first paragraph?' 'That used to be true at one time', Ryle replied. 'I had a lot more time in those days.'

A grandson of the first Bishop of Liverpool, Ryle was himself an atheist – but he was what he called 'a singing atheist'. He used to distinguish between those atheists who would join in hymns in church, and those who, if forced to attend a service, would keep their mouths tightly shut throughout. A lifelong bachelor, he was thought by some to be too unemotional to be a convincing philosopher of mind. 'Do you ever read any novels, Ryle?', a critic once asked him. 'Yes', he replied, 'I read all six of them every year.' He did indeed have a great admiration for Jane Austen, and once wrote a sensitive piece about her morality.

Unlike many Oxford philosophers, Ryle had a good knowledge of continental philosophy, and early in his career he had written a respectful review of Heidegger. While convinced of the superiority of analytic methods, he made more than one attempt to bring the two traditions into contact with one another, organizing what might be called interfaith conferences, one at Royaumont Abbey and one in Oxford. But his brusque Anglo-Saxon style put off some of the continental philosophers, and German visitors in particular were not pleased to be told that the great merit of analytic philosophy was that it made no claim to 'führership' in philosophy.

One of Ryle's last publications was a speculative biography of Plato. The character of Socrates, dominant in Plato's early dialogues, is diminished, and is sometimes totally absent, in the later dialogues of his old age. Ryle explained this on the basis that the dialogues were intended for public performance, and that Plato himself acted the part of Socrates. If so, it was natural that the character should disappear when Plato, in old age, lost his teeth and could no longer perform. *Plato's Progress* was not taken very seriously by the learned world, but Ryle did not seem to mind.

## Richard Hare, philosopher

When I became a Balliol tutor my senior colleague was R. M. Hare, who was then the dominant figure in British moral philosophy. After the logical positivists had downgraded ethical judgements to little more than expressions of emotion, he reminded the philosophical world that practical and moral thinking had its own genuine logic. In *The Language of Morals* (1952), he pointed out that there is a logic of imperatives no less than a logic of assertion, and he drew on this to expound a theory of moral reasoning. He distinguished between prescriptive and descriptive meaning. A descriptive statement is one whose meaning is defined by the factual conditions for its truth. A prescriptive sentence is one which entails, perhaps in conjunction with descriptive statements, at least one imperative. To assent to an imperative is to prescribe action, to tell oneself or others to do this or do that. To make a moral judgement is to issue an imperative which applies universally, to oneself as to all others in similar situations.

Hare distinguished between ethics and morals. Ethics is the study of the general features of moral language, of which prescriptivity and universalizability are the most important. Moral judgements are prescriptions and prohibitions of specific actions. In principle, ethics is neutral between different and conflicting moral systems. But this does not mean that ethics is practically vacuous: once an understanding of ethics is combined with the desires and beliefs of an actual moral agent, it can lead to concrete and important moral judgements.

During the years that we were colleagues at Balliol I had many philosophical discussions with Dick Hare. He was one of the most formidable intelligences I have ever encountered. During that time, I do not remember ever once winning an intellectual argument with him. We often walked along the sodden towpaths of the Thames, where he took unfair advantage of his enormous height, launching a challenge just before striding across a puddle with his long legs, leaving me to think of an answer as I splashed through the muddy water, two steps to his one. His ethical system was already well entrenched, and he was skilled at anticipating and turning aside any criticism I could devise. I found it more rewarding to discuss with him neutral philosophical topics such as the nature of time, where his sharp mind operated free of the constraints of publicly adopted battle lines.

As my senior, with many years of college experience, he was generous with advice on many topics. When he heard that I was thinking of getting married, he told me, 'Too many people spend time experimenting with different sexual partners. My advice is to find the right woman, and the sex will look after itself.' He himself had an utterly delightful wife and a happy family of four children. When I first took a group of students to the Alps, he and his wife accompanied me to show how to organize a reading party – they had long experience of running such events in England.

The student who suggested to me on that occasion that I should take a reading party was, in fact, Dick's son John, who became a lifelong friend – though we see each other rarely because he teaches at Yale. We once together walked up Pike's Peak in Colorado. The hike takes you to the altitude of Mont Blanc, but arrival at the summit is an anticlimax because it is covered with a vast car park surrounding a hamburger joint.

John is the author of several books, in one of which he seeks to introduce a religious element into his father's moral philosophy. The venture seems to me unsuccessful. It is true that, as a young man, Richard Hare wrote an essay which argued that without faith in God, philosophy can never be a serious occupation – only a game.

But he never published that essay, and in his published work one has to labour to detect any religious element at all. There is no entry for 'God' in the index to *The Language of Morals*. What remained of the earlier faith, to judge by the published works, was a conviction that the world was such as to make morality viable, an attitude which could perhaps be called faith in Providence. Throughout his life, his son tells us, Hare attended Anglican worship regularly, and used to recite the creeds. In my own discussions with him I found it hard to tell how far he accepted the content of those creeds. To those who asked him if he was a Christian, his standard response was, 'I don't know. I'll tell you what I believe, and then you tell me whether you count me a Christian or not.'

In 1965, Hare was appointed to the Oxford Chair in Moral Philosophy, which was attached to Corpus Christi College. His departure left a vacancy in Balliol to which we appointed a New Zealand philosopher, Arthur Prior, who had invented tense logic. Arthur knew no Greek, so he took my place as a PPE tutor while I took over Dick's responsibility for the Greats students. I also moved into the teaching room he had occupied at the top of Balliol's winding, turreted, staircase III. Long and narrow, the room contained an enormous sofa on which Dick had every day taken his constitutional siesta after lunch, always strictly limited to half an hour.

Because he was now a professor, on a university rather than a college payroll, Dick had to vacate his college house. He said that trying to buy a house was one of the worst experiences of his life: 'I had no idea that there were so many wicked people in the world!' This from a man who, as a prisoner of the Japanese, had worked on the Burma Railway!

Hare's ethical system attracted few wholehearted disciples, but several other influential philosophers – including Bernard Williams and Alasdair MacIntyre – developed their own views in explicit or implicit reaction against that system. He had an exaggerated idea both of Oxford's importance in the world of philosophy, and of his own importance in the world of Oxford. 'We in Oxford', he once wrote, 'are content to be the heirs of Plato and Aristotle.' When it was suggested to him that he should publish some of his papers alongside those of his most eloquent Oxford critic, Philippa Foot, he refused to do so on the grounds that he had no wish to confer immortality on that lady's ephemeral essays. Fifty years on, Foot's philosophy has worn better than his own.

## Philippa Foot, philosopher

Philippa Foot's maiden name was Bosanquet, which linked her to a nineteenth-century British Idealist philosopher, and among her ancestors was the US President, Grover Cleveland. Once, as a student, I took my mother to listen to her give a lecture. I doubt if she appreciated much of the moral philosophy, but she was entertained by Philippa's old-fashioned upper-class diction as she listened to her dropping the final 'g' in words like 'hunting' and pronouncing 'burglar' as 'burgular'.

Philippa was introduced to me by her colleague at Somerville, Elizabeth Anscombe. Though in terms of college hierarchy she was the senior of the pair, being a fellow while Elizabeth was a mere lecturer, Philippa always deferred to Elizabeth's philosophical judgement. This seemed to me quite natural, given Elizabeth's talents. I soon began to notice, however, that in discussion with me too, Philippa would behave as if I were the serious thinker and she were the novice. It dawned on me that self-deprecation was her normal manner of philosophizing, and that beneath it there was intense intellectual determination.

It was as an opponent of R. M. Hare that Foot first made her name as a moral philosopher. In her lectures, she would point out the futility of using some chilly formal criterion as the mark of a moral principle. No amount of prescriptivity or universalizability would make it a moral judgement that one should always put on the right shoe before the left one. Morality must link up in an intimate way with human nature. Humans are the kind of being who need the virtues if they are to thrive, in the same way as plants need water in order to flourish. She pointed out that it was astonishing that there was no entry for 'happiness' in Hare's *The Language of Morals*. By the omission, he cut himself off from a grand tradition in moral thinking going back to Plato and Aristotle.

On her own account, however, it was the reading of Aquinas that first made Foot suspicious of the fact–value distinction on which Hare and his colleagues placed so much weight. She and I had many discussions on Aquinas' theory of double effect – that is, the idea that if an act has both good and bad effects, it may be permissible provided that the bad effects are only foreseen and not intended. Foot was initially rather suspicious of the doctrine. She criticized it in an article in which she discussed whether the driver of a runaway tram would be right to steer it down a track where one man was sure to be killed, rather than an alternative track where five men would be killed. This example became famous, particularly in America, where it was known as 'the trolley problem'.

Over the years, Foot became more sympathetic to the doctrine of double effect – partly, I hope, as a result of our discussions, both in person and on paper. But personal meetings became rarer after 1969, when she resigned her Somerville tutorship and began to freelance in America. From 1976 to 1991 she was a full professor at UCLA, and spent time in Oxford only in vacations.

One shared experience with Philippa recurs frequently in my imagination. In 1975, the two of us were attending a conference in Dubrovnik in circumstances I will explain in a later chapter. We took a day off to visit Mostar to see the spectacular high-arched medieval bridge across the Neretva river. We had to hire a taxi as, in those days, there was no public transport, and we found the town virtually deserted. No one spoke English, and the two of us were totally unable to read signs in the local language. So we had to spend half an hour in silence outside the public toilets, waiting for someone else to make use of them so that we could tell which were for males, and which for females.

This trivial event came to mind when I paid my next visit to Mostar in 2016, many years after the bridge had been destroyed during the civil war and rebuilt with UNESCO aid. The town was so crowded that one had to fight one's way on to and over the bridge; there were notices in English everywhere; and the beautiful arch was disfigured by a huge wooden contraption to enable tourists to dive into the depths of the river.

After Philippa's death, I read the collected letters of Iris Murdoch and learned of the long-standing love affair between the two women. I was taken by surprise, as I had always imagined Philippa's attitude to sex as prim and conservative. As often, I encountered the difficulty of really understanding the personalities even of those one loves and believes one knows well.

# 9

## Three Wittgensteinians

### Elizabeth Anscombe

In the 1950s, the English Dominicans used to organize an annual gathering of Catholic philosophers at their priory at Spode in Staffordshire. It was there that Herbert McCabe introduced me to a remarkable couple – Elizabeth Anscombe and Peter Geach. It quickly became clear to me that the two were the most talented philosophers in the Catholic community, and they were generous of their time in discussion. While Peter taught philosophy at Birmingham, Elizabeth at that time was a college lecturer at Somerville. She was one of the literary executors of the great philosopher Ludwig Wittgenstein, and in 1953 she had published the English translation of his posthumous *Philosophical Investigations*.

The first lecture series I attended when I went to Oxford as a graduate philosophy student in 1957 was a course on Thought and Action given by Stuart Hampshire. He began by telling us all to read Miss Anscombe's recently published *Intention*. It was indeed the publication of this book which established her as an influential philosopher in her own right. Her account of the nature of one's knowledge of one's own intentional actions, and her development of Aristotle's discussion of practical reasoning, set the terms of several debates that continue to the present day.

Anscombe had already become famous in Oxford, but not for theoretical philosophy. In 1956, the university offered an honorary degree to the US president who had authorized the bombing of Hiroshima and Nagasaki. Anscombe opposed the proposal, arguing in a pamphlet, 'Mr Truman's Degree', that it was monstrous to honour a man responsible for two massacres. She set out the doctrine of the just war, as developed long ago by Catholic theologians such as Suárez and Protestant jurists such as Grotius. According to that doctrine, nothing could justify the deliberate killing of non-combatants in war.

Anscombe did not succeed in persuading her fellow dons: only four people voted against the conferment of the degree. Surprisingly, however, the theory of the just war – which had been almost totally forgotten during the 1939–45 war – has gradually become accepted, not only in ecclesiastical circles but also in official and military ones. In the last decade, for instance, several of the cardinal principles of that doctrine were enunciated in the counter-insurgency manual issued by General Petraeus to the US forces under his command. The revival of the theory, I believe, is due more to Anscombe than to any other individual.

As a graduate student, while still a priest, I began to see a great deal of Elizabeth, who was warmly welcoming to graduate students with a serious interest in philosophy. She kept open house at 27 St John Street: one could drop in at any hour of day or night and start a discussion of a philosophical problem. Elizabeth had a houseful of children, to whom she would attend from time to time, but that did not interrupt the flow of philosophy. She was also, in those days, a chain-smoker, dropping her butts into a huge wooden bowl. It was only in later years, as a tutor myself beset with the enthusiasms of young graduate students, that I came to appreciate fully the generosity with which she made herself available.

Among my many memories of these discussions, one stays in my mind. A fellow student who also enjoyed discussions with Anscombe was Tom Nagel. One evening, trying to understand the Catholic opposition to artificial contraception, Tom put the question: 'Elizabeth, would it be sinful if I were to play the piano with my penis?' There was a long pause, and then Anscombe said slowly 'An und für sich – No.'

Elizabeth had an earthy side: she frequently used four-letter words, and from time to time would give me graphic accounts of various aspects of sex that she thought I needed to know about when hearing confessions, and about which she believed (rightly) I was not well informed. She was famous for having defeated C. S. Lewis in debate, and that had left him with a grudge against her. He once told my Oxford landlord – a fellow member of a drinking group,

Alexander Jones, General Editor of the Jerusalem Bible, surrounded by his circular bookrest, 1966

Staff and students of the English College, 1950. Jack Kennedy is immediately behind Cardinal Griffin, and Cormac Murphy-O'Connor is the tallest person in the top row

Elizabeth Anscombe and Peter Geach in 1993: a formidable philosophical couple
Steve Pyke; courtesy Getty Images

Philippa Foot in 1993: a moral philosopher whose writings have stood the test of time
Steve Pyke; courtesy Getty Images

Christopher Hill after unveiling, in Balliol, his portrait by Derek Hill

Harold Macmillan with the author on the steps of Balliol Hall

Ted Heath and George Malcolm attending a Balliol Musical Society concert

Roy Jenkins enjoys a joke

President Cossiga, between the author and the President's aide, on a visit to Oxford

To Sir Anthony Kenny
with thanks for a great day
Bill Clinton

Bill Clinton at Rhodes House, 1996

Peter and Jonathan Brooke at the Balliol cricket pavilion

Hillary Clinton with the author and his wife, Nancy Kenny

called the Inklings – that she had once publicly asked him, 'When did you last masturbate?' I once plucked up courage to ask Elizabeth whether the story was true. She denied it, but admitted that in the course of a truth game she had put the question to him, and to the other players, 'What is your most disgusting personal habit?'

The most educational experience of my life was attending the evening seminars in a run-down annex of Somerville in which Anscombe inducted us into Wittgenstein's argument against private ostensive definition. From time to time, she would single me out as a spokesperson on behalf of the idea of private language, and then gradually demolish everything I could say in its defence. It was a painful experience – the intellectual equivalent of defoliation by wax – but immensely rewarding. I gradually came to understand what Wittgenstein meant and to see why it was important. As a result of her seminars I found my whole mindset altered, so that every philosophical problem looked different from the new perspective I acquired.

'D'you know, Tony', Elizabeth once said to me, 'I don't have a single idea in my head that wasn't put there by Wittgenstein.' The remark was revealing, but wholly inaccurate. In the first place, there were the ideas that were put there by her husband, Peter Geach, who had been teaching her long before she met Wittgenstein. Obviously, Geach and Anscombe had a great influence on each other; but as philosophers they operated quite differently. Anscombe was the better tutor, Geach the better lecturer and much the better writer. Geach was more influenced by Aquinas and by Frege than he was by Wittgenstein. He could take offence when people asked him what his wife thought on a philosophical topic, and assumed that he knew and agreed with whatever it might be. 'As her husband', he used to say, 'I have privileged access to her body, but not to her mind.' In the second place, Anscombe's head was full of Catholic thoughts that were at some distance from the ideas of Wittgenstein. At a different time she said to me, 'On the topic of religion, Wittgenstein is sheer poison.'

As a graduate student, I was never officially supervised by Elizabeth. It was she, however, who suggested to me the topic of my dissertation – namely, the intentionality of psychological verbs. The topic was approved by the philosophy sub-faculty, and I was assigned Anthony Quinton as my supervisor – the beginning of a lifelong friendship. Elizabeth gave me access to appropriate unpublished papers of Wittgenstein, and Quinton was a wonderful guide to contemporary philosophical literature.

I left Oxford to take up a curacy in Liverpool without having finished my dissertation. However, I was able to send drafts to Oxford for Elizabeth and Peter to read, and they were most encouraging about it. Elizabeth told me that they felt a sense of disappointment when it was concluded and there was no more of it to read: 'Othello's occupation's gone', she said, not very appropriately.

In 1961, I returned briefly to Oxford to defend my dissertation on intentionality. The thesis was examined by David Pears and Patrick Gardner. As I mentioned in Chapter 3, viva voce examinations are theoretically public in Oxford, but rarely attract an audience. Surprisingly, Elizabeth turned up to listen to mine. Her presence seemed to disconcert the examiners no less than myself. Fortunately, they retained enough composure to accept the dissertation, which was later published as *Action, Emotion and Will*.

In 1959, the Oxford Chair of Logic fell vacant. After a stormy meeting, which led both Austin and Ryle to resign from the electoral board in protest at the way the vice chancellor had conducted the election, A. J. Ayer was appointed. Anscombe was disgusted: 'We've already had Ayer in Oxford', she said to me. 'We don't need him again.' In public discussion the two were willing to be quite rude to each other, as in the legendary exchange: 'Professor Ayer, if you didn't speak so fast, people wouldn't think you were so very clever.' 'Miss Anscombe, if you didn't speak so slowly, people wouldn't think you were so very profound.'

During my time as a curate in Hall Lane, Liverpool, I more than once went to stay with the Geachcombes. I stayed in the house in St John Street, where no door was ever locked. When I took a bath, Elizabeth would come and sit on the edge of it to continue a philosophical discussion. I stayed also in Elizabeth's rustic farmhouse in the Shropshire hills – the Foxholes. Life there was primitive, and one was dependent on an open-air privy illustrated with primitive frescoes of the Last Judgement. Elizabeth tried to teach me to ride a horse. She placed me on a well-tempered mare – but two of her children unlocked the door of the stable where the stallion was kept, and I had to cling on for dear life as the mare fled headlong from his approaches. I was put off riding for ever. It was while driving one of Elizabeth's sons to Foxholes that I caught from him the infective hepatitis that caused me to be moved from Hall Lane to Crosby.

I wrote from Liverpool to confess to Elizabeth that I was suffering grave doubts about the Catholic faith. She responded with great generosity to my confession of faltering belief, and we corresponded for months about the nature of knowledge, certainty and faith. We also had an exchange of daily postcards arguing for and against the existence of God. But this was not sufficient to restore my faith. I came to think that the right thing for me to do would be to seek laicization. She told me that this would make no difference to our friendship: 'You are the kind of friend', she said, 'whose good is our good, and harm to whom is harm to us.'

When, after laicization, I went back to Oxford, we resumed our close philosophical friendship. While I was a philosophy tutor at Balliol, I gave a number of joint classes with Anscombe, and we benefited from the flexibility of Oxford tutorial arrangements to exchange students. I sent some of my most promising Balliol under-graduates to her, and she allowed me to give tutorials to some of her brightest Somerville students. I was approached by Random House to write a book about Descartes. 'Why would anyone want to write a book about Descartes?', I asked Elizabeth. 'His whole system could be written on the back of a postcard and he had only two ideas, both of them wrong.' 'If that's what you think about the great man', she replied, 'you had better write a book about him to teach you better.' I did, and was indeed brought to a sounder mind.

Elizabeth was a feminist, but one of an unusual kind. She resolutely refused to change her name on marriage, and letters to Mrs Geach were returned unopened. But she was hostile to any concessions being made to women as women. One week, a delinquent student made some stammering excuse in a tutorial for not having written the week's essay. 'Let me show you what I've been doing since last week', Elizabeth said, and produced a five-day-old baby.

Sadly, our friendship came to an abrupt end. Elizabeth reacted with indignation when, in 1965, I told her that I planned to get married without a papal dispensation: 'Our dearest wish for you', she said, 'must be that you will be desperately unhappy in your marriage.' Thus excommunicated, I hardly saw her again for many years, until I found myself doing business with her as a fellow trustee of Wittgenstein's literary estate.

## Peter Geach

It was through my friendship with Elizabeth Anscombe that I first got to know Peter Geach, while I was a graduate student in Oxford. As a lecturer in Birmingham, he was only at home at weekends, and was absent for most of my student meetings with Elizabeth. But when I returned to Oxford as a fellow of Balliol, Peter had a double reason for making friends with me, because he had a great affection for that college, where he had spent his undergraduate years in the 1930s.

In his old age, Peter would often say that Balliol had saved his immortal soul. He meant this literally. His father, a philosophy professor in the Indian Education Service, was a man who constantly changed his religion. (When he was a schoolboy at Clifton College, friends would greet Peter after the vacation with, 'Hullo Geach! Good hols? Does God exist *this* term?') One of Geach *père*'s mystical experiments was devil worship, of the style promoted by Aleister Crowley. He encouraged his teenage son to join him in this supernatural quest. It was arriving at Balliol in 1934, Peter would later explain, that cured him once for all of any temptation to indulge in such pernicious nonsense.

Whether or not this is true – and it must be confessed that, as he got older, Peter's memory became more and more creative – it is certain that his years as a Balliol undergraduate had a lifelong influence on his intellect and his character, and left him with a passionate, indeed romantic, love for the college. His childhood had been unhappy: his father's marriage to Eleonora Sgonina, the daughter of Polish emigrants, had broken up shortly after his birth, and when he was four years old he had been made a ward of court and was forbidden to have contact with his mother. Years at Llandaff Cathedral School and Clifton College left little mark: it was at Balliol that, for the first time, Peter found himself in congenial company.

Like many another Balliol man, he owed far more to his contemporaries than to his tutors. In 1991 he wrote, in a preface to a Festschrift:

> Apart from the healthy immersion in Plato and Aristotle that I owe to my tutor, Donald Allan, I owe far more to Balliol for the freedom of endless discussion with my peers than for any formal philosophical teaching. In retrospect I seem to have spent four years almost entirely in Balliol; I never went to philosophy lectures outside the college and knew hardly anybody in other colleges.

In Peter's Balliol years, 1934–8, there were certainly many interesting undergraduates to converse with. When he arrived, Jo Grimond and Stuart Hampshire were already in residence; George Malcolm and John Templeton were his exact contemporaries; and during his years in college Edward Heath and Denis Healey arrived. In the last years of his life, Peter was one of the very few survivors of that fascinating pre-war generation.

It was in his final year, just before gaining a first in Greats, that Peter became a Roman Catholic. In his later memoirs, he attributes this above all to discussion with his Balliol contemporaries. He wrote of his Balliol years:

> Increasingly, as time went on, I found myself arguing with Catholics. I was certainly cleverer than they, but they had the immeasurable advantage that they were right – an advantage that they did not throw away by resorting to the bad philosophy and apologetics then sometimes taught in Catholic schools. One day my defences quite

suddenly collapsed: I knew that if I were to remain an honest man I must seek instruction in the Catholic Religion.

An event in Peter's undergraduate career that entered into college legend took place on 11 December 1936, the day of the abdication of King Edward VIII. With the help of a freshman history under-graduate, Hugh Fraser, Peter raised a Jacobite flag above the Balliol tower and proclaimed the accession to the throne of the Stuart pretender, Rupprecht of Bavaria. Recording this event later, he explained that at the time, influenced by Hobbes, he had believed that it would be in the nation's benefit to restore a strong monarchy:

> No such thing could be hoped for, I thought, so long as the House of Windsor reigned; I judged them to be quite unfitted, by character, tradition, and training, to assume the role of Sovereign, instead of rubber-stamping Acts of Parliament. Only romantic folly made me ignore the question whether the family who would be *de jure* claimants if the Hanoverian usurpation were undone were at all likely to be better as Sovereigns.

When recalling in private his Jacobite escapade, Peter would observe tartly that their joint venture had not prevented Sir Hugh Fraser (Secretary of State for Air, 1962–4) from 'serving as Minister to the Guelph usurper'.

Peter detested the political philosophy of the Oxford of his day which praised Locke and Rousseau and condemned Hobbes. Hobbes is often regarded as the father of British empiricism, but Geach placed him elsewhere in the history of thought. He once wrote to me:

> Hobbes belonged to a splendid tradition of Tory politics: I count in a sort of English apostolic succession the following persons (all male): Saint Thomas More, Hobbes, Dr Johnson, William Cobbett, G. K. Chesterton. What a galaxy of fine old eccentrics, who wrote so well!

I think he would not have objected to being regarded as a successor to that tradition. Geach had been brought up by his father to despise the logic then taught in Oxford by the likes of Cook Wilson and F. C.

S. Schiller, and he saw no reason, later in life, to revise that opinion. Only his reading of the *Nicomachean Ethics* with Donald Allen seems to have left a positive, lifelong influence. It was only after leaving Oxford that he began the reading of Aquinas that exhibits itself prominently in much of his later work.

It was at Blackfriars on Corpus Christi Day in 1938, just after his success in Greats, that Peter met his future wife: 'He massaged my shoulder', Elizabeth told me, 'and said, "Miss Anscombe, I like your mind."' It was to be three years before they married, but from that moment they forged one of the most fruitful philosophical partnerships of the twentieth century. Peter, in a memoir, offered a moving description of the years between their engagement and their wedding:

> Elizabeth had a lot of philosophical teaching from me. I could see that she was good at the subject, but her real development was to come only under the powerful stimulus of Wittgenstein's lectures and her personal conversations with him. Naturally she then moved away from my tutelage; I am afraid that I resented that, but I could recognize this feeling as base and irrational, and soon overcame it.

When war broke out, Peter, like Elizabeth, became convinced that the British government would not observe the rules of just war, and for that reason he became a conscientious objector. He was willing to serve in the Polish army, but his attempts to do so were unsuccessful, so he spent the war in timber production.

Geach went on to become one of the dozen best British philosophers of the twentieth century, and to become a master of English philosophical prose second only to Thomas Hobbes, John Henry Newman and Bertrand Russell. He retained a lifelong devotion to Balliol, and was delighted when elected to an honorary fellowship in 1979. I still recall the debate in governing body when he was proposed for election. There were those who were opposed: Geach was too much of a Catholic apologist, and there were other famous Balliol philosophers, X and Y, who had a stronger claim. The issue was settled when an atheist philosophy fellow growled, 'Geach's writings will still be read when X and Y are names that everyone has forgotten.'

Many legends circulate about the unconventional style of the family life at 27 St John Street. Some of them are very likely true. Here, I will repeat the only story on the topic that I had from Peter himself. Some neighbour had reported them to the NSPCC for cruelty to their children. When the inspector arrived, it was explained to him that one of the boys had indeed been beaten for breaking some precious object. According to Peter, the inspector, having surveyed the damage to the treasure and the damage to the boy, decided that what had been inflicted was merited and proportionate.

When I first knew the Geachcombes, Peter was much the more ferocious member of the couple. He could work himself into a rage at some foolish intervention in a philosophy seminar, and Elizabeth would have to go up to the podium to soothe him down. But over the years the dynamics between the two changed, reversing the direction of a similar change that overtook Macbeth and Lady Macbeth. In their old age, it was Elizabeth who was the more belligerent, while Peter achieved a degree of serenity – occasionally interrupted by bouts of mental illness. This showed itself, for instance, in his attitude to my marriage. He did not exhibit the hostility to it that Elizabeth had shown, and after her death, Nancy and I several times visited him in the Cambridge home where his children took turns in looking after him. Once he said to me, 'Tony, are you still faithful to Nancy?' 'Er, yes, as a matter of fact', I said, rather taken aback. 'I am glad to hear that. It makes me believe that it was genuine intellectual reasoning that took you out of the Church. You aren't like Brentano [a philosophical ex-priest of the nineteenth century] who got through several wives in a decade.' At our last meeting before he died, Peter startled me by saying, 'You are just like Wittgenstein.' 'In what way?', I asked. 'Like him, you hang on to God by the thinnest possible thread.'

In his sixties, Geach wrote an autobiographical poem in elegiac couplets. It has not been published, and I doubt it ever will be. But it contained two lines which, written when he was sixty-nine, and quoted at the funeral service after his death at the age of 97, are a wonderful summary of his serene old age:

> Sexaginta annos complevi hucusque novemque,
> In Domino sperans, dum vocet ipse: Veni.*

## Georg Henrik von Wright of the Academy of Finland

In his will, of 29 January 1951, Wittgenstein bequeathed to Rush Rhees, Elizabeth Anscombe and Georg Henrik von Wright 'all the copyright in all my unpublished writings; and also the manuscripts and typescripts thereof to dispose of as they think best'. These heirs were to publish 'as many of my unpublished writings as they think fit', and were to share the royalties and other profits equally between themselves.

Wittgenstein's heirs reflected three different aspects of his own character. Von Wright, a logician and philosopher of science, corresponded to the austere and technical philosophy of Wittgenstein's early *Tractatus*; Anscombe was the most suitable proponent of his late philosophy of mind; and Rhees had an affinity for the mystical streak in his early and late thought.

The legacy placed a heavy burden on the heirs. Because of Wittgenstein's inability to bring his work into a form he thought suitable for publication, a vast quantity of material of great philosophical value remained unpublished at his death. Each of the heirs was assigned an initial task: Anscombe was to edit and publish the *Philosophical Investigations*, von Wright was to published selections from Wittgenstein's work on the foundations of mathematics, and Rhees was to edit the *Big Typescript*, the nearest to a conventional book that Wittgenstein had produced in his lifetime.

The work of the first two heirs was well received, but when, in 1970, Rhees published a highly edited version of the *Big Typescript*

---

\*  'Sixty years and nine have I lived until now, but I await, hoping in the Lord, for the day when he calls me: "Come!"'

under the title *Philosophische Grammatik*, it was widely criticized. Of the heirs, Rhees was the one I knew least, but I got to know him briefly when I was commissioned to prepare an English translation of the *Grammatik*, which appeared in 1974. While working on the text, I visited Rhees in his house in Swansea from time to time to discuss translation problems. There he lived alone, guarded by a massive German shepherd dog that would place his paws on the shoulders of incoming visitors. I became aware that the text Rhees had published, on the basis of a certain stage of Wittgenstein's own revisions, was only one of many possible orderings that could claim Wittgenstein's authority. The chief fault of Rhees' published text was that it gave no indication at all of the amount of editorial activity that lay behind it. Cuts were made silently, and transpositions merely hinted at; important material in the *Typescript* was simply omitted.

In the course of translating Rhees' text I drew up a full account of the editorial decisions he had made, along with their justification – when there was one – in Wittgenstein's papers. I wished to put this as an introduction to the English version, but Rhees forbade it on the ground that it would 'come between Wittgenstein and the reader'. Eventually I presented my account as a separate piece entitled, 'From the Big Typescript to the Philosophical Grammar.' I published this in a Festschrift for von Wright in 1976. By this time, he had become the one of the trustees whom I knew and loved best.

Georg Henrik was a Swedish-speaking Finn who had studied in Helsinki in the 1930s under the logical positivist Eino Kaila, before studying under Wittgenstein and eventually succeeding him as Professor of Philosophy in Cambridge in 1948. Those who met him always had difficulty with the pronunciation of his surname. Should it be pronounced 'von Frickt', as continentals always did, or 'von Ryte', as some Anglophones preferred? When I once asked him, Georg Henrik told me that the Anglicized pronunciation was correct: he was descended from a seventeenth-century Scotsman called Wright, who had migrated to Germany and there been ennobled.

Before I first met him, I had read his works with admiration. He was renowned for his work in modal logic (the logic of possibility and necessity) and had invented a parallel discipline of deontic logic (the logic of permission and obligation). Two works of moral philosophy – *Norm and Action* and *The Varieties of Goodness* – were classics of analytic philosophy. Of all Wittgenstein's disciples, he was the one who retained a completely independent style of thought and writing.

It was because of the troubled history of the Wittgensteinian *Nachlass* that he and I became good friends. In 1989, Rhees died. For some time, the trustees had been giving thought to the future of the *Nachlass* after their death, and each had privately nominated a successor: Anscombe nominated Anselm Müller of Trier, Rhees nominated Peter Winch, and von Wright nominated myself. For quite a while, these nominations were kept secret from the persons involved. Soon after Rhees' death, however, Peter Winch became a trustee, and in spring 1990, I was invited to join the trust, von Wright having decided that he would wish me to do so before he had ceased to be a member of the board. From this point, the proceedings of the trustees became more formal, with roughly annual meetings minuted by a secretary who, from 1991 until his death, was Winch.

For ten years I used to meet Georg Henrik at meetings of the Wittgenstein trustees. These were sometimes held at Trinity Cambridge, Wittgenstein's own college, of which Georg Henrik was now an honorary fellow. Sometimes they were held in Helsinki, or another Nordic city. And, on one or two occasions, they were held in my own Oxford residence, Rhodes House.

Entertaining the von Wrights was a pleasure, but it also put hosts on their mettle. Their mere presence enforced certain standards of polite behaviour from a bygone age. Georg Henrik, a most pacific person, bore himself with an upstanding military presence. His wife, Elizabeth, concealed a warm and generous heart beneath a stern patrician exterior. Georg Henrik must have been one the last people I have known who could be described, as a compliment and without irony, as a perfect gentleman.

I soon discovered that my main function as a trustee was to keep the peace between Anscombe and von Wright. They disagreed over many aspects of the publication of Wittgenstein's works, and if Georg Henrik was a gentleman, Elizabeth was anything but a lady. During this period, there were several abortive attempts at a publication of the complete *Nachlass*. The most contentious of these was a project that had been started in 1975 by a team under the direction of Michael Nedo and Professor H. J. Heringer of Tübingen, with financial support from the Fritz Thyssen Foundation.

Sadly, the project was a failure. Though about half the *Nachlass* was transcribed into a computer, not one volume of text was published during the lifetime of the project. The collaborators quarrelled, and the Tübingen Wittgenstein archive was dissolved. Nedo moved from Tübingen to Cambridge. He and Ms Isabelle Weiss began a new project for a complete transcription of the posthumous writings into a database. In 1981, the then trustees applied to an Austrian government research foundation for support for the Nedo project. The years went by, and by the time I became a trustee Nedo had still not produced any publishable text. Instead, he devoted much of his time to designing software to produce a particular page layout. My first meeting as a trustee resulted in Nedo being given an ultimatum: he would receive no further support from the trust unless he produced four volumes by May 1991. The deadline came and went, and nothing appeared.

Meanwhile, however, Anscombe, despite the collective decision of the trustees, continued to support Nedo, and eventually – 20 months later – Nedo presented the trustees with six volumes ready for the printer. These were published a few years later under the title *Wiener Ausgabe*. The edition received no authorization from the trustees, and remained incomplete.

A more successful publication of the *Nachlass* resulted from cooperation between the University of Bergen, and Oxford University Press. In 2000, four CDs were produced which contained facsimiles of all the manuscripts, plus two scholarly printed texts. The edition sold widely, and despite some imperfections it has broadly satisfied scholars' needs for access to Wittgenstein's legacy. But until his dying day, I think Georg Henrik regretted that it was available only in electronic form, rather than in a *Gesamtausgabe* of handsomely bound volumes.

In 1996, Elizabeth Anscombe was involved in a serious car accident and suffered injuries to the head. In succeeding years she suffered occasional periods of disorientation, and this sometimes made it difficult to conduct the business of the Wittgenstein Trust. I had, by now, acquired a thick skin in relation to Elizabeth, but Georg Henrik was more sensitive and lost much sleep as a result of the difficulties of dealing with her.

In 1997 Peter Winch died, and at a meeting of all the trustees in the following year, two distinguished Wittgenstein scholars, Peter Hacker and Joachim Schulte, were elected to join the board. After the meeting, Elizabeth, whose concentration and memory were already beginning to fail, denied that she had consented to their appointment, and raised various objections. So during the last years of her life it was impossible to hold meetings of the trustees.

Early in 2001, I wrote to Georg Henrik to narrate the story of Elizabeth's death and burial. I reported that after a requiem Mass in Blackfriars, Cambridge, Nancy and I had accompanied the family and a dozen other mourners to Ascension Parish Burial Ground, where Wittgenstein was buried. Though the cemetery was officially closed, Elizabeth had secured special permission from ecclesiastical lawyers to be buried beside Wittgenstein: they dug her grave at twice the usual depth to leave room for Peter, who was eventually buried there after his death in 2013.

I ended my letter by pointing out that it was now once again possible for the trustees (including those recently appointed) to convene. We did so in October 2001, in von Wright's house in Helsinki, and agreed, without friction, on future policy for the publication of Wittgenstein's works. It was the last time I saw Georg Henrik, for he died in 2003. On his death, the trust was wound up, and the Wittgenstein papers passed into the control of Trinity College, in accordance with terms set out by the original heirs in a trust deed of 1969.

Georg Henrik used to say that alongside the austere rationality of his early work, he had always fostered another side of himself – one interested in *Weltanschauung*, rather than analysis. As he grew older, these concerns came to the fore. He began to wonder whether the form of rational thought which he had once regarded as supreme was having negative repercussions upon life as a whole, and in particular its aesthetic and cultural aspects. His latest writings, such as *The Tree of Knowledge* (1993), echo this solemn and gloomy note. He even began to think that his invention of deontic logic had been a mistake.

In Finland, von Wright was always regarded with profound reverence, not only by academics but by the general public. He was given a special research professorship by the Academy of Finland, among other national honours. His letters and working papers are now among the most treasured possessions of the country's national library. I am proud that my own long correspondence with him is among the material that has found its home there.

# 10

# Three overseas philosophers

## Willard Van Orman Quine

Having spent many a sabbatical term lecturing in US universities, I have made friends with many American philosophers, but four of them stand out. I will briefly mention the first three – Davidson, Plantinga and Kretzmann – before moving on to the main subject of this essay: Quine.

Soon after I joined the philosophy teaching staff in Oxford, I had a visit from a professor in Stanford whose name was quite new to me. He was Donald Davidson, who had just, comparatively late in life, switched disciplines from psychology to philosophy. He told me that he was writing a review of my first philosophy book, *Action, Emotion and Will*, and we had a lively discussion of my treatment of the logic of adverbs. Donald never finished that review, but the work he was doing turned into a series of articles on human action that had a far greater impact than anything I ever published on the topic. He and I kept in touch over the years, and one year I invited him to a reading party at the Saint-Gervais chalet, where the group spent ten days discussing his philosophy. We planned to ascend Mont Blanc together once the students had departed, but the weekend we had set apart for the ascent was totally blanked out by rain at our level, and snow at every upper level. Later, he was a visiting professor in Oxford, and I enjoyed watching the debate in seminars where he was pitted against the champion local philosopher, Michael Dummett.

In 1973, I took part in a summer institute on philosophy of religion at Calvin College, Grand Rapids. Peter Geach and I were invited to lecture to a young faculty brought together from small and isolated colleges. The presiding presence was Alvin Plantinga, who from the tiny department at Calvin had established a formidable international reputation. He was a hero to the conference from the first day: a tall, blond, handsome, athletic, second-generation

Friesian. He gave courses in mountain climbing, and his lecturing technique was very like his alpine one: first, make quite sure of the position you are in before taking a step, then take it swiftly and confidently. The three weeks of that conference amounted to one of the happiest philosophical experiences of my life, and the beginning of a wonderful friendship. Like Davidson, Plantinga came to the chalet to spend time discussing his work with my students. Once again, my guest and I kitted ourselves out for the ascent of Mont Blanc, only to be thwarted by the weather.

Since then, I have enjoyed many a hike with Al on his visits to England. I was delighted when, in 2017, he was awarded the Templeton Prize for making the academic world take seriously the philosophy of religion. He is famous for his Free Will Defence to the problem of evil, and for having flogged new life into the ontological argument for the existence of God.

Norman Kretzmann and I were brought together by our interest in medieval philosophy. Norman came from Cornell University to Oxford for a year to work with Arthur Prior on medieval logic. Sadly, Arthur died just after he arrived, and I had to serve as a poor substitute. Gradually, Norman's interests spread beyond logic to broader issues of medieval philosophy, in which I could be of help to him. With the help of Jan Pinborg of the University of Copenhagen, Norman and I edited a massive *Cambridge History of Medieval Philosophy*. In the summers of 1979, 1980 and 1981, the three of us met for two-week editorial conferences at Cornell University, copy-editing texts that had been submitted, and chasing up delinquent contributors. Norman had been brought up a Lutheran, and was descended from a long line of Lutheran pastors, but he lost his faith, and for most of his life was an atheist. Shortly before his death he recovered an austere, non-confessional belief in God. This was the result of a decade's work on Thomas Aquinas, in which he undertook a critical commentary on the *Summa contra Gentiles*.

Three years after the commencement of the work, Norman was diagnosed with multiple myeloma, and the doctors gave him a year to live. In fact, he survived for seven years, and worked on the commentary to the last days of his life, publishing two volumes with OUP in 1997 and 1999. A few weeks before his death, I said to him, on the telephone, 'You are treating your illness very philosophically.' 'Of course', he replied, 'I have a PhD in that subject.'

During my philosophical career, the towering American figure has been W. V. O. Quine. The founding fathers of analytic philosophy were the Cambridge professors, Bertrand Russell and Ludwig Wittgenstein. After their death, Oxford was briefly the world centre of analytic philosophy; but in the latter part of the twentieth century, the centre of gravity of the movement was in America. The shift can be dated to 1953, when Quine came over from Harvard for a year to hold a visiting professorship. He punctured the complacency of the Oxford professors. John Austin recorded this in a verse that became famous:

> Everything done by van Quine,
> Is just fine.
> Why can't he leave us alone,
> To fossick around on our own?

By the time I began to teach philosophy, Quine was generally regarded not only as the top American philosopher but as the world leader of the analytic movement. As a young don, I was very impressed by his books *From a Logical Point of View* and *Word and Object*, though I could never accept the view of philosophy expressed by them. I had learned from Wittgenstein that philosophy and science are two totally different disciplines, science seeking to discover facts and philosophy seeking to achieve understanding. Quine, having attacked the distinction between analytic and synthetic truths in an early essay, saw philosophy simply as a fringe activity continuous with science.

I don't think that Quine ever took me seriously as a philosopher. He never mentions me in his books, and when we used to meet in the houses of philosopher friends he would always steer the conversation on to general topics. Conservative in his views, he detested the student fashions of the sixties and seventies. And he would have no truck with 'democracy in the classroom', which meant giving everyone an A grade without respect to performance. Seeing a sophomore wearing a T-shirt with the slogan 'It doesn't matter what you believe, as long as you're sincere', he quipped: 'It should read, "So long as you are not sincere".'

I could never share Quine's belief in the omnicompetence of natural science, a dogma he inherited from the logical positivists of the Vienna Circle. In *Word and Object*, he insisted that there was no logical bridge from the propositions of natural science to the language of intentionality in which we ascribe meanings and attitudes to our fellow humans. He adopted a double standard: when we are on our best behaviour we should avoid the indirect-speech constructions we use to describe people's thoughts and intentions, and confine ourselves to scientific descriptions of physical states and reaction. I agree with Peter Geach – a good friend, but severe critic of Quine – that this is an absurd self-denying ordinance, though I do not follow Geach's argument that the gulf between scientific and intentional language is a proof that God creates each individual human soul.

Though we were far apart in our fundamental view of philosophy, Quine was always a model of academic courtesy to me. Each time he published a new book, he would send me a copy with a friendly autograph inscription. I now have a fine collection of signed copies of his later works, which I treasure.

There was one topic of philosophy on which I totally agreed with him. In the latter part of the twentieth century, the harmless logical discipline of modal logic – the logic of necessity and possibility – spawned a noxious metaphysic of possible worlds. Quine mocked this at its very foundation. In his paper of 1951, 'On What There Is', he wrote:

> Take, for instance, the possible fat man in that doorway; and again, the possible bald man in that doorway. Are they the same possible man, or two possible men? How do we decide? How many possible men are there in that doorway? Are there more possible thin ones

than fat ones? How many of them are alike? Are no *two* possible things alike? Is this the same as saying that it is impossible for two things to be alike? Or, finally, is the concept of identity simply in-applicable to unactualized possibles? But what sense can be found in talking of entities which cannot meaningfully be said to be identical with themselves and distinct from one another?*

The questions asked by Quine seem to me unanswerable, and thus to expose the incoherence of the notion of unactualized possible individuals. I reject his reduction of the intentional to the physical, but wholly endorse his reduction of possible worlds to the actual world.

## Ernst Tugendhat

When first I took to philosophy, there was a sharp divide between analytic and continental philosophy. This was viewed with some complacency in Oxford, since we regarded analytic philosophy as unquestionably superior. But some continental philosophers realized, sooner than we did, that it would be a good idea to bring the two traditions together. One of these was Ernst Tugendhat of Heidelberg. In 1970 I invited him, with a colleague, to join my first reading party in our alpine chalet. He accepted with enthusiasm, and he had a permanent effect on my reading parties since he insisted, with German precision, that minutes ('protocols') should be taken of each night's philosophical debates, to be subsequently approved at the commencement of the following night's discussion.

Ernst came to the chalet more than once. He was a skilful but demanding chef: if there was a particular spice he thought essential for a dish, he would send a student four thousand feet down to purchase it in the valley. He was also a gifted portrait photographer, and in old age I am grateful to him for providing me with haunting images of long-dead friends.

---

\* W. V. Quine, *From a Logical Point of View* (Cambridge, MA: Harvard University Press, 1963), p. 66.

Over the years, Ernst visited Oxford several times, and got to know most of the leading Oxford philosophers. He wrote a number of books aimed at bringing together the diverse philosophical schools, and spotted early on that a good way to do so was to focus on the philosophy of Aristotle, which had fed into both traditions.

It was in 1972 that I was most closely connected with Ernst. As a sabbatical project, I was due to translate the posthumous work of Wittgenstein's, *Philosophische Grammatik*, into English. I was happy with my grasp of the philosophical thrust of each paragraph, but not confident enough of my German to publish a translation without having a careful eye cast over it by a native speaker. I wrote to Ernst, offering to spend my sabbatical in Heidelberg and teach some courses to his students if he would agree to vet my translation.

In Heidelberg, my wife and I and our two young sons moved into an apartment in the newly completed university guest house, supported by a British Academy fellowship. Each week I produced my quota of translation pages; at the weekend, Ernst came round to go through the text with me, correcting my errors and explaining passages that had left me baffled.

Ernst's assistance was the more remarkable because that year was a very trying time for him. The student revolution had gone much further than it ever did in Britain: for instance, after each lecture by a professor, a student would give a counter-lecture pointing out the professor's bourgeois errors, and contrasting them with the true Marxist position as seen by the students. The extraordinary thing was that these counter-lectures were funded out of the university budget by the Social Democratic government in Baden-Württemberg.

Tugendhat was in a specially difficult position. He was dean of the faculty, and he was caught in the middle between radicals in Heidelberg and the Kultusministerium at Stuttgart. At one time, threatened by revolutionaries, he needed an armed guard on his house; at another, he was reprimanded by the Kultusministerium for making a concession to the students which was disapproved of. It was an extraordinary act of kindness – in those circumstances – to spend so much time helping me with my translation.

## Jacques Derrida

If Ernst Tugendhat provided me with a link to German philosophy, there was a time when I hoped Jacques Derrida might provide me with one to French philosophy. One of my philosophical colleagues, Alan Montefiore, spoke English and French, and was anxious to link the philosophers of both languages. He arranged a number of exchange visits between Oxford and the École normale supérieure in Paris. I see, from my diary, that Derrida visited Oxford in February 1968, November 1969, and May 1970, while we Oxford visitors paid return visits in between. Sadly, this series of exchanges ended abruptly in 1970. The École normale caught the disease of student power later than other Paris institutions, but it caught it in a particularly virulent form. In the aftermath of the Paris *événements*, riotous students at a *bal prolétarien* burned part of the École's library, and the funds that had been used for exchanges had to be diverted to repair the damage.

At the time of the exchanges, Derrida was not yet famous as the founder of deconstructionism, but had made a name for himself with his *Of Grammatology*. Our discussions were not easy: I had read that work, and he had read my *Action, Emotion and Will*, but we could not make much of each other's writings. The most rewarding form of communication was for us to read closely together the text of some philosopher we both revered, such as Descartes.

It was many years before I met Derrida again, and in the interval he had been corrupted by becoming famous. He gave up philosophy for rhetoric, and rhetoric of a particularly childish kind. As his career developed, his style of operation moved far away, not only from current analytic philosophy, but from philosophy as understood by the great philosophers from Aristotle to Husserl. It has always been seen as a task of the philosopher to draw distinctions between concepts that may be confused with each other, and if necessary to invent or adapt terms to mark these distinctions. Derrida, by contrast, introduced new terms whose effect was to confuse ideas that are perfectly distinct.

The later Derrida maintains the reader's attention by the deft deployment of rhetoric. A particularly successful device might be named 'The Irrefutable Paradox'. One of the most quoted lines in *Of Grammatology* – underlined by the author himself – is, 'There is nothing outside the text.' An arresting, even shocking remark! Surely the Black Death and the Holocaust were not textual events in the way that a new edition of Johnson's *Lives of the Poets* is a textual event. But later Derrida kindly explains that, by text, he does not mean a corpus of writing, but something that overruns the limits of the world, of the real, of history. Well, if what we are being told is simply that there is nothing outside the universe, it would be rash to contradict. And an injunction to try to see things in context is surely sound advice.

Like the skilful rhetorician that he is, Derrida keeps his readers awake by bringing in sex and death. Talking to oneself, we are told, stands in the same relation to talking aloud as masturbation stands to copulation. No doubt it does. A no less apt comparison would have been with solitaire vs whist: but that would not have tickled the reader in quite the same way. Again, at the end of the book of Revelation, we read: 'And the Spirit and the bride say, Come! And let him that heareth say, Come' (22.17). Derrida has written at length on this text, making great play with the double entendre that attaches, in French as in English, to the word 'come'. If one were churlish enough to point out that the Greek word for 'come' cannot possibly have the sense of 'achieve orgasm', one would no doubt be told that one had missed the whole thrust of the exercise.

It may appear unseemly to criticize Derrida in the manner just illustrated. The reason for doing so is that such a parody of fair comment is precisely the method he adopted in his own later work: his philosophical weapons are the pun, the bawdy, the sneer and the snigger. Derrida himself rejected the idea that his work can be incapsulated in theses, and sometimes even disclaimed the ambition to be a philosopher. It is unsurprising that his fame has been less in philosophy departments than in departments of literature.

# 11

## Three prime ministers

### Harold Macmillan

In my first term as a fellow of Balliol, Harold Macmillan was the guest of honour at the college's annual feast on St Catherine's Day, 25 November. He gave an eloquent speech, finely balanced between comedy and tragedy. Beginning with reminiscences of his undergraduate days, he recalled that his Greats tutor had told him, 'Nothing that you will learn in the course of your studies will be of the slightest possible use to you in life – save only this – that if you work hard and diligently, you should be able to detect when a man is talking rot. And that, in my view, is the main, if not the sole, purpose of education.' He would then enlarge the subject beyond the college walls, quoting the words of Ronnie Knox: 'We in Balliol should never take a narrow and provincial view of the universe. We should imitate the genial tolerance of the sun which rises over Wadham and sets over Worcester.' Then there came the solemn part of the speech, when he recalled that for years after the war ended in 1918, he did not dare to set foot in Oxford because it was a city only of ghosts, so many of his contemporaries having been killed in battle.

It was an oration I was to hear many times in the years to come. I continued to admire it, and to find it both amusing and moving. As I moved up high table and came to sit close to the great man, I was astonished to find how nervous he became as the moment for his speech approached: he would fall silent, toy with his food, and become oblivious to the remarks of his neighbours. But once launched into speaking he would regain confidence and once again deliver a most professional performance.

I got to know Macmillan after I became Master of Balliol. As Chancellor of Oxford University, he often had to attend functions in various colleges. For many years, he had stayed on these occasions at All Souls with the Warden, John Sparrow, but he did not find those lodgings congenial after Sparrow's departure: 'Can't move anywhere without meeting young ladies with tennis rackets', he complained, referring to the daughters of Warden Neill, whom he nicknamed, rather unfairly, Mr Quiverful. Henceforth, when he had to spend a night in Oxford he would stay in the guest room of the old Master's lodgings in Balliol, and though I now lived with my family in a different house, the King's Mound, I always spent the night in the next room when he was there.

If he took dinner in Balliol, he used to sit on for hours in the senior common room surrounded by dons, students and old members. At midnight or one, he used to progress across the quad to the drawing room in the lodgings, and he and I would gossip alone for another hour or two over a glass of Scotch. We were both admirers of Anthony Trollope and Ronald Knox, and as the night drew on he often spoke as if I too could remember the golden Edwardian years of Balliol. We did not much discuss present-day politics. I once ventured to ask him what was the truth about his alleged responsibility for handing over Cossack prisoners to be massacred by the Russians at the end of the war. He put his hand over his eyes and said, 'I can't recall anything about it. It was all so long ago.'

In 1981, I joined Macmillan in performing a somewhat bizarre duty. When the Prince of Wales became engaged to Lady Diana Spencer, we learned that Oxford University was one of half a dozen Privileged Bodies with the right to present a loyal address to the sovereign on the occasion of the marriage of the heir to the throne. The chancellor, vice chancellor and other senior academics were deputed to do so: I was included in the deputation on the grounds that I happened to then be the chair of the Association of University Teachers, the academic staff's trade union. When the ceremony took place in Buckingham Palace, I was the last to be presented to Her Majesty by Chancellor Macmillan. Scorning any briefing that I was there as a trade unionist, he said, 'And now, Ma'am, I have the honour to present the head of the finest college in Oxford – my own college of Balliol.'

In 1985, there came the day when the dons of Oxford University voted down a proposal to give Mrs Thatcher an honorary degree.

Roy Jenkins used to relate the story that when the news of the refusal broke, Macmillan buttonholed him in a corridor in the Commons and said, 'How embarrassing that our university should insult the prime minister in this way! How disgraceful!' At this point, according to Jenkins, Macmillan's tone changed and his eyes sharpened: 'You know, it's all really a matter of class. The dons are upper middle class and the prime minister is lower middle class. But you and I, Roy, with our working-class backgrounds, are above that kind of thing.'

Of all the Macmillan dinners in Balliol, the most memorable took place in 1986. During an official visit to Britain, the General Secretary of the Communist Party of China, Hu Yaobang, expressed a wish to visit Oxford. It was decided that he should be entertained in Balliol as the guest of the chancellor. Our bursar and staff were quite experienced at laying on dinners for grand guests, but the Foreign Office decided that food and drink were not enough. There must also be a display of British culture, and they laid on a team of actors and musicians to entertain the guests for an hour after dinner, with a celebration of 11 ages of man.

The occasion was not a happy one. The chancellor seemed to get on well enough with the aged Hu Yaobang, but I found myself next to Li Peng, the Chinese premier. My feeble jokes over dinner went down badly, even after heavy editing by the interpreter. After dinner, by the time we got to the third age of man, our guests were visibly impatient. Macmillan leaned behind his neighbour to whisper to me, 'Can we not summon the proctors' men and eject these strolling players?' A hapless university official was sent to negotiate with the entertainers. They agreed to cut the 11 ages to six. Jeremy Irons, the lead actor, bounded down the steps saying he had never been so insulted. The Chinese guests leaped into their official cars the instant the actors disappeared.

When, later in the year, Macmillan became terminally ill, I was one of the last of his Oxford friends to visit him on his deathbed in Birch Grove, Sussex. I represented Oxford at his funeral, and read the lesson from First Corinthians at his memorial service in the university church. But the memory of him which I most cherish dates from an earlier period. Normally Macmillan was an early riser, even after a long midnight session over whisky. But one day he decided to stay in bed in the lodgings until noon. As it happened, on that day I was giving a pre-lunch party in honour of the musician George Malcolm, an honorary fellow of the college. Halfway through the party Macmillan appeared in a dressing gown, and quickly became the centre of attraction. As the guests began to depart, he looked around the room with sober satisfaction. 'What a magnificent scene of debauchery', he said, 'Master – chancellor all unbraced – empty champagne bottles as far as the eye can see.'

## Ted Heath

When Ted Heath became prime minister in 1970, there was much excitement in Balliol. Heath had been an organ scholar in the college, and had remained a loyal alumnus, often persuading his friends among first-rate musicians to perform at Balliol Sunday night concerts. But the then Master of the college, the Marxist historian Christopher Hill, was guarded in his approach to the new prime minister. He sent a telegram from the senior common room: 'Political congratulations from some of us, personal congratulations from all of us.' While Hill was in charge, Heath received no invitation to the college.

Shortly afterwards, however, Hill went on sabbatical, leaving in charge a South African mathematician, Jack de Wet, who had been a contemporary of Heath's at Balliol. Jack seized the opportunity to invite Heath to dine with the fellows in the SCR. Between the issuing of the invitation and the actual dinner, the Conservative government signed an agreement for strategic cooperation with South Africa, thereby making Heath a target for anti-apartheid demonstrators. On the morning of the prime minister's visit, it was discovered that graffiti had been painted on several college walls, and the great plate glass windows of the SCR had been inscribed with 'Fuck Heath' in large letters. The bursar and his staff worked hard to clean everything up in time for the dinner, but it was clear that the meal was likely to be disrupted. The dean of the college had to summon 20 police from the Special Branch to escort the guest of honour across the quadrangle from the Master's lodgings, where we had taken sherry, to the SCR, where we were to dine.

It was while we were crossing the quad, amid violent scuffles between police and demonstrators, that I had my first encounter with Heath. We found ourselves walking side by side: 'This is a new experience for us', I said, 'but I expect you're quite used to this kind of thing.' 'Never seen anything like it before in my life', was his reply. But during dinner, he chatted urbanely and energetically, as if nothing untoward had happened. Rather sententiously, I explained to him that many of the fellows were not supportive of his policies, but that one could enjoy dinner with someone with whom one strongly disagreed. 'Of course there are limits', I went on to say: 'I wouldn't have accepted an invitation to a meal with Hitler.' 'Oh, wouldn't you?', said Heath: 'I once did, in the 1930s.'

I cannot recall any further meetings with Heath during the mastership of Christopher Hill, but when I became Master myself he displayed a lot of affection for the college, and in my first year established a Heath Junior Research Fellowship. During the Thatcher administration, ten years after the 'Fuck Heath' demonstration, the demonstrators returned to the college for their first gaudy. The fellow who welcomed them back remarked in his speech that the sentiments they had painted on the windows were now more often to be heard within 10 Downing Street.

On his visits to the college, Heath made no secret of his antipathy to Mrs Thatcher. Arriving on one occasion, he barked: 'D'you know what that woman wants to do now? She is trying to remove my bodyguard!' At the time, the IRA did indeed present a threat to senior politicians, but I felt that what outraged Heath was less the loss of security than the loss of dignity. I was reminded of Lear's lament when his daughters strip him of his hundred knights.

Heath managed to retain his bodyguard, but he was not always well served by it. To mark the centenary of the Balliol Musical Society he persuaded Yehudi Menuhin, Janet Baker, George Malcolm and the Lindsay String Quartet to give a special concert in the college hall. He and Menuhin occupied adjacent rooms in the lodgings on the occasion. The close protection officer confused the two men's suitcases, and only by making a last-minute dash to Heath's car did I save Menuhin from having to perform without trousers.

As part of the memorial concert, Heath himself conducted a chorus of Balliol students – the chapel choir, reinforced by a number of volunteers. They did not seem to have enjoyed the experience. Can it possibly be true that he conducted the Liebeslieder Waltzes four beats to the bar?

While my wife and I were glad to welcome Heath back to college, he was notoriously difficult to entertain. The conventions of placement meant that, at dinners, he often sat next to Nancy rather than to me, and she found conversation quite a strain. Owing to some malady, Heath would fall asleep at table during a gap between sentences. Nancy, when first due to entertain him, had been warned by a senior hostess of her acquaintance, 'I prepared three topics to discuss – sailing, music and politics. We had used them all up by the time we reached the soup.'

When Harold Macmillan died in 1986, there was much speculation in Oxford about possible successors to the chancellorship of the university. I was pleased to learn, early on, that Roy Jenkins was willing to stand – but shortly after that, I was told that Ted Heath also intended to let his name go forward. I was saddened by this; I had become fond of Ted, and admired the magnanimity he had shown to Balliol, but I was sure that he had no real chance of being elected, and did not want to see him wounded again after all he had suffered under Thatcher. I approached several of his close friends, urging them to dissuade him from standing, but to no avail.

Since Jenkins and Heath were both honorary fellows of the college, Balliol's governing body decided to remain officially neutral between the two, and offer each of them, impartially, such assistance as they might require from the college office. The vice chancellor of the day, Patrick Neill, secured the nomination of a third candidate,

Lord Blake, the Provost of Queen's College, believing that he would be seen as a non-political academic. In fact, Blake was seen as the Thatcherite candidate, and was supported by those who had been outraged by the university's refusal to give the prime minister an honorary degree.

Most of the fellows of Balliol, as individuals, were supporters of Heath. The Labour dons would naturally not vote for Blake, and many had not forgiven Jenkins for defecting from their party in 1981 to found the Social Democrats. In the final days of the election, instructions came from Downing Street that Conservatives should vote for Heath, rather than Blake; but despite this last-minute switch, Jenkins won easily.

When the result was declared, Ted was taking tea with his supporters in our lodgings. Our teenage son Charles was deputed to run from the Proctors' Office to communicate the result as soon as the votes were counted, and it fell to him to announce the news of Ted's defeat. Writing a day or two later, I tried to console Ted by telling him that if the electorate had been restricted to the fellows of Balliol, rather than to the Congregation of the university, he would have been chancellor by a large majority.

After I ceased to be Master and moved to Rhodes House I would meet Ted from time to time at Balliol functions, to which we were both invited as honorary fellows. Ted continued to call me 'Master' for years after I had ceased to hold the job. One day in the buttery I said, 'Ted, please call me "Tony". If you keep on calling me "Master" I'll have to start calling you "Prime Minister". 'Oh, I would like that!', was his reply.

During our time at Rhodes House, Nancy and I used to invite Rhodes Scholars to dinner, a dozen or so at a time, where they would be addressed by a specially invited guest of honour. Ted agreed to fill this role on a day in 1991, which turned out to be just after George Bush senior launched the first Gulf War. The Scholars had been addressed the week before by Sir Patrick Mayhew, the attorney general who had advised the government on the legality of the war. Heath spoke out strongly against the decision to go to war – Kuwait was not a proper nation, he maintained, and did not deserve to have us put our troops in harm's way: 'And I ought to know', he said, 'because I helped set it up.'

More than once, Ted invited Nancy and me to Sunday lunch in his beautiful house in the Cathedral Close at Salisbury, whose gardens backed on to rivers on both sides. One of the guests we met there was Sara Morrison, with whom I had worked years earlier on a committee to discuss Anglo-Irish affairs (see Chapter 15). She was, I believe, Ted's closest woman friend, and he would accept criticism and advice from her that he would not have taken from anyone else. When Ted died, I wondered for a while where I should direct a letter of condolence. I decided that Sara would be the most appropriate person, and in her reply she said that I had probably guessed rightly.

Ted's death left me with one puzzle. For many years, each summer, two hundred pounds would mysteriously appear in my bank account. I could never discover where it came from, or for what purpose it was supposed to be used. All I could discover was that it was paid through Brown Shipley. The payment ceased the year after Ted died; and when his biography appeared, I learned that Brown Shipley was his private bank. I continue to wonder whether, among his other eccentricities, it was his habit to send anonymously holiday money to his friends.

## Margaret Thatcher

Oxford University has traditionally offered an honorary degree to those of its alumni who have become prime minister. But, notoriously, in 1986, Congregation, the university's parliament, refused to honour Margaret Thatcher. It is often said that the proposal for an honorary degree would have been uncontroversial if it had been put forward by Oxford's Hebdomadal Council when she first became prime minister in 1979. Not so. I was a member of that Council in 1979. When Thatcher became prime minister, there was immediately consideration of the award of an honorary degree. After keen discussion, Council decided not to put a proposal forward: she had made herself too unpopular because of the recent increase in fees for overseas students. It would be dangerous to put her name forward and then have it rejected by the university's Congregation: that would be the worst of all possible worlds.

We decided to wait until the prime minister became more popular. We waited, and we waited, and then at last the time seemed ripe. Those of us who had previously opposed the proposal were converted by Thatcher's behaviour during and after the Brighton bombing. We admired her personal courage at the time, and the magnanimity she showed by continuing the quest for peace in Northern Ireland. In Council, I proposed that the university should send her a message of congratulation on her escape, and I was among those members who, late in 1984, voted to put her name forward for the degree.

However, between Council's proposal and the decisive vote in Congregation, two things happened. First, it was proposed to abolish free tuition for British undergraduates. When that measure was withdrawn because of pressure from backbenchers, the loss to the Treasury was made up by raiding the science budget. Hence, between October 1984 and January 1985, two new constituencies of anti-Thatcherites were recruited, who combined to vote down the proposal for an honorary degree.

I have been told – I know not on what authority – that Thatcher was so incensed by Balliol's part in the campaign against the honorary degree, that she blocked a proposal to award me a knighthood. Certainly, it was only after John Major became prime minister that I received the honour that normally comes up with the rations when a commoner is elected as President of the British Academy. But on the rare occasions when I met her personally, she was always friendly and charming.

The first such occasion was at the time of the official visit of Hu Yaobang. I was invited to Downing Street on the Tuesday before he came to Balliol, no doubt so that I could learn how to entertain the august guests. I took the opportunity to consult Denis Thatcher about the Foreign Office proposal for an evening of cultural entertainment.

'Get it stopped', he said. 'I have done this job for seven bloodstained years, and I can tell you that the last thing you want is an hour of culture late at night in a language you don't understand.' Next day, I telephoned the Foreign Office to tell them that their proposal had been countermanded in Downing Street – but it did not take them long to see through the ruse.

Several years later, when Thatcher was no longer prime minister, and I had left Balliol for Rhodes House, I hosted a dinner there to celebrate the opening of the Saïd Business School in Oxford. I was placed next to her, and we had a lively discussion about the Rhodes Scholarships. While prime minister, she had worried that the Marshall Scholarships, funded by the British government, were less well regarded than the Rhodes Scholarships, funded from the will of Cecil Rhodes. Ambassadors had tried to reassure her that, in intellectual terms, the Marshall Scholarships were superior to the Rhodes Scholarships. 'You mean to tell me', she said, 'that we are spending all this money to produce a bunch of academics?'

So, on that evening in Rhodes House, she sent me off from the dinner table to fetch a copy of Cecil's will. I presented it to her, and watched in silence while she read through it. When she got to the point where the will specified that the Scholars were not to be mere bookworms, her eyes lit up. 'How right he was!', she said.

# 12

## Three British statesmen

### Denis Healey, Chancellor of the Exchequer

I had only two encounters with Denis Healey, but both were dramatic. The first was in 1983 when Balliol was celebrating the septcentenary of its refoundation by Dervorguilla. Denis attended the celebrations and stayed in our lodgings. He always maintained that a serious politician should have a hinterland – a set of non-political interests. At dinner at high table, he exhibited the breadth of his own hinterland: he quoted stanzas of poems in several languages, and challenged the neighbouring dons to follow on and complete the poems. He entertained the other guests with character sketches of foreign politicians – 'In any normal country, Andreotti would be in gaol' – and, in particular, with the story of a recent Vatican money scandal. That had led, by devious routes, to the suicide or murder of the financier Roberto Calvi, found hanging from Blackfriars Bridge. An officer of Denis' acquaintance in the CID had reconstructed the crime by buying a rubber woman from a sex shop in Soho and blowing her up at the scene of the death. It was not quite clear how this assisted in the detection, but Denis kept the audience fascinated as he narrated his friend's story.

In 1985, Healey was the guest of honour at the college's annual St Catherine's Day Dinner, a feast attended by both senior and junior members. It was the tradition on these occasions to pass a silver loving cup from hand to hand and mouth to mouth for the diners to drink the toast, *Floreat Domus de Balliolo*.* The year was at the height of the AIDS scare, and some dons worried whether it would be safe to continue the tradition of the loving cup. I consulted the chaplain and the college doctor. The chaplain told me that there was no case known of AIDS being spread by the use of the communion

* 'May the house of Balliol flourish.'

cup. The doctor said that, though there were 17 diseases you could catch from a loving cup, AIDS was not one of them. Accordingly, I instructed that the cup was to be passed round as usual.

Rashly, over the course of dinner, I told Denis of the inquiries I had made, and the reassurances I had been given. Denis made an excellent speech, but as it was drawing to a close he said: 'And now it is time for the loving cup. The Master tells me that there is a one in seventeen chance of catching AIDS by drinking from it, but such is my trust in the Master's heterosexuality that I am happy to share it with him.'

Next day, of course, I received angry letters from gay and lesbian groups protesting about the insult to their sexuality, and demanding that Denis be stripped of his honorary fellowship. A year later, the minority groups took their revenge. Stephen Twigg – later to be famous for his surprise capture of the Enfield Southgate constituency from Michael Portillo in the 1997 general election – proposed, and got passed, a motion forbidding heterosexual 'frolicking and pseudo-affectionate activity' in the JCR.

In the years just before the war, Denis Healey and Roy Jenkins had been contemporaries at Balliol and had been made honorary fellows after parallel careers of distinction in the Labour Party. In 1981, however, Roy left the party, as one of the Gang of Four, to found the Social Democratic Party. Naturally, this led to a breach with Denis. Roy told me that the two of them met on a train while campaigning for their respective parties. As they took their leave of each other, Denis gave a loud shout: 'The worst of luck, Roy!'

## Roy Jenkins, Lord Jenkins of Hillhead

It was just after he left the Labour Party that I first met Roy. In March 1981, Nancy and I gave a party in the lodgings to celebrate the foundation of the Social Democratic Party (SDP). Several dons entertained hopes that this new party's leader might become the fourth twentieth-century Balliol prime minister. But by the time Harold Macmillan died at the end of 1986, the SDP was defunct, and

Roy's own ambitions had taken a gentler form. He put his hat in the ring to succeed the great man as chancellor of the university.

For a while, it looked as if Roy would be a shoo-in, and I was looking forward to joining the campaign on his behalf. But against the advice of his friends, and without the support of the Conservative Party, Ted Heath announced his intention to stand, as I recalled in the previous chapter. Heath's support came largely from the Left, especially from members of the Labour Party who had not forgiven Roy's defection to the SDP, and who did not approve of his social activities. 'We can't have as chancellor', one economist said at a college meeting, 'a Balliol man who goes around screwing duchesses.'

The election went to an exciting finish when, at the last minute, Downing Street advised Conservative members of Congregation to vote for Heath, rather than Blake. However, the two Balliol candidates seem to have had a premonition of the outcome. The college offered premises for post-election parties. Heath booked the Master's drawing room for a tea party of 24. Roy ordered evening champagne for 80 in the Old Common Room.

When the votes were counted, Roy scored 3,429 votes, Blake 2,674, and Heath 2,348. Journalists delighted to point out that under a system of proportional representation – for which Roy was a great advocate – he would have been defeated in the second round by a combination of the Conservative votes. In his autobiography, Roy devoted a not wholly convincing paragraph to arguing that he would have won, even on an alternative vote system.

Once installed by the first-past-the-post system, Roy stepped into Macmillan's shoes with remarkable aplomb, and became a very popular chancellor. When conferring honorary degrees in the annual Encaenia ceremony he would take great pains with his Latin pronunciation, marking the stresses on his copy of the text, and rehearsing in advance with the public orator. During his chancel-lorship he conferred degrees by diploma on more than a dozen heads of state, including, most conspicuously, President Clinton. It gave him great satisfaction to receive visiting monarchs in his capacity as the democratically elected head of a modest academic republic.

Roy was frequently invited by colleges to attend their feasts, and to open new buildings. He calculated that, in 1987, he fulfilled 73 engagements in Oxford. He never played hard to get, and he put himself on record as not once having declined a serious invitation to dinner. 'God forbid', a journalist quipped, 'that Lord Jenkins should ever receive an unserious invitation to dinner in Oxford.'

The serious invitations, of course, carried with them the obligation to give a speech. Roy took considerable pains over preparation, telephoning round his friends to make sure his information was correct, and to try out the epigrams he had moulded for the occasion. Inevitably, there was a certain amount of repetition between one speech and another. He loved to quote a passage from *The Idea of a University* that celebrated the Oxford colleges' 'umbrageous groves'. Old hands in the audience, hearing the name of Newman, would cock their ears to hear how, this time, the chancellor would cope with the pronunciation of those two prominent 'r's.

The conventions of placement meant that Roy's immediate neighbours at high table were often women. He was a model of respectful gallantry to those he found attractive and intelligent, but on occasion could make it embarrassingly clear that he felt he had been ill placed. He was once positively rude to a dear friend of mine – so much so, that he had to follow up with a letter of apology. I did not see the letter, but I was given the impression that it was on the lines of 'Dear Lady X, Jennifer tells me that I must apologize to you and that you are not at all as stupid as you look.'

Besides formal occasions, Roy enjoyed informal conviviality. After his death, Robert Harris wrote:

> If British politics and letters are the poorer for Roy's passing, so too, it must be said, are the landlords of the Blue Boar at Chieveley, The Harrow at West Ilsley, the Royal Oak at Yattendon, the Red House at Marsh Benham, The Fish at Sutton Courtenay, the White Hart at Hamstead Marshall, and a large number of other congenial establishments spread across Oxfordshire and West Berkshire.

Roy had a policy of never taking lunch alone, and he built up concentric circles of lunching companions. Harris was a member of the inner circle, who shared his lunch every fortnight. Nancy and I were not so privileged, but we belonged to the monthly group. We were also frequently guests at the house in East Hendred where Jennifer and Roy dispensed generous hospitality at weekends, and we became good friends with their son Charles and his warm Croatian wife Ivana. Every New Year's Day, the Jenkinses came to our house for brunch, where they were star guests.

Conversations with Roy were always delightful, whether they were on politics, history or literature. He and I were both keen fans of Anthony Trollope. His favourite of the political novels was *The Duke's Children*. He told me that that novel had been the favourite also of Macmillan and of Churchill. It occurred to me that the novel was about the emotions of an elder statesman coping with the coming of age of his three children, and that Jenkins, Macmillan and Churchill had all lived through that experience.

When Tony Blair became prime minister, Roy had great hopes of him. It was not just that Blair had succeeded, where Roy had failed, in moving the Labour Party towards the Centre. For a while, the new prime minister treated Roy as a guru, asking his advice on constitutional reform and other issues. This phase did not last long, but in one area Roy did have an effect on policy: he pointed out that financial cuts were seriously threatening the prestige of Britain's great universities. The University of Salamanca, he told Blair, used to be one of the most celebrated universities in the world, and had now faded from global consciousness. Unless a remedy was applied soon, Oxford might share the same fate. This conversation was one of the things that led – for better or worse – to the government allowing universities to charge their students substantial fees.

In his final illness, Roy was treated in the John Radcliffe Hospital, and Jennifer spent some time in our house, which was nearby. In our last conversation, Roy spoke very highly of the consultant who was treating him, whom he had consulted about how safe it was to drink. 'You must be very careful', the consultant said, 'you must drink neither more nor less than you usually do.' Roy thought this sound advice, and lined up behind the curtain a row of half-bottles of claret. He asked me whether it would be possible to get a college fellowship for the excellent consultant.

After Roy's death, Nancy and I continued to see a lot of Jennifer, walking with her from time to time in the Downs or in the Chilterns: we often found it hard to keep up with her, even though she was many years older than either of us. We talked often about Roy's biography. Andrew Adonis had been appointed by Roy as his official biographer, but he was kept busy by his own energetic political career. In the end, he had to give up the task. It was a pity that he had not done so earlier, when the eventual biographer could have had more time to inspect the papers in East Hendred and interview ageing comrades. After many discussions of possible biographers, Jennifer settled on John Campbell, who produced a fine volume in 2014. The party to launch the book was a memorably irenic affair. One could see David Owen fraternizing with men who thought he had wrecked the SDP, and Jennifer embracing women who had been revealed in the book as Roy's mistresses.

Jennifer asked me to chair a committee to raise money for a memorial to Roy. Unkind people said that the most appropriate memorial would be free claret in cardiac wards, but we decided to establish instead a set of scholarships to bring to Oxford students from the European Union. In a short time we raised half a million pounds, and the scheme was launched in 2003. That endowment proved sufficient, during the years before the scheme was wound up in 2017, to bring to Oxford some 80 scholars from the EU who were proud to bear the name of a man who had been both Chancellor of Oxford and President of the European Union. By that time, the first ever Jenkins Scholar, Michal Bobek, had risen to be Advocate General at the European Court of Justice.

When Peter Hennessy's book, *Cabinets and the Bomb*, was published in 2007, I learned that at the time when Roy was home secretary, there was a plan, in the event of government being incapacitated during a nuclear attack, for a destroyer to take into the ocean the Queen, Prince Philip, their private secretary and Roy. Four privy councillors, it seems, is the quorum necessary for the nation to be governed. When the book appeared, I asked Jennifer what she thought of the story. 'A load of nonsense', she said. 'But perhaps', I persisted, 'Roy never told you because he was sworn to secrecy.' 'Rubbish', was the reply. 'Roy was extremely good at telling me things he was not supposed to tell anybody.'

## Chris Patten, last Governor of Hong Kong

Because Chris Patten read history rather than philosophy, I have no recollection of meeting him when he was an undergraduate at Balliol, though he was in his final year when I became a fellow. But to this day, Chris likes to tell the story of discussing an essay at an early tutorial with the medievalist Maurice Keen. 'Charlemagne', the essay began confidently, 'can be regarded as the ultimate founder of the European Union.' 'I b-b-b-beg your pardon', responded the startled Maurice.

My first memory of Chris was when, as a young MP, he attended a dinner along with Harold Macmillan and Ted Heath. Ted several times tried to persuade the senior statesman to denounce the policies of Mrs Thatcher. Macmillan would respond quite promisingly – but then change direction at the last minute and avoid any actual criticism of the prime minister. Chris Patten likened his behaviour to that of a Victorian dowager who would pull up her dress to reveal a shapely ankle, and then promptly lower it again.

At that time, Chris himself was no great fan of Mrs Thatcher. I recall him denouncing a fellow MP for taking office in her government – 'and all for a buckle on his shoe'. But, in 1983, he became parliamentary undersecretary for the Northern Ireland Office, where his Catholic background stood him in good stead during the peace process. It was when he was Minister for Overseas Development, from 1986 to 1989, that our paths crossed again: he was most helpful when David Astor and I were organizing the Southern African Advanced Education Project. In 1989, as Secretary of State for the Environment, he was given the thankless task of steering through Parliament the legislation imposing the poll tax.

At the time of the general election of 1992, Chris was chair of the Conservative Party. He organized the party's national victory, while losing his own seat as MP for Bath. By that time I was on sufficiently friendly terms to be able to write to him that I wished that he had kept his seat, and his party had lost the election. A close ally of John Major, he was consoled for his disappointment by being sent as Governor of Hong Kong, the last Briton to hold that post.

At this period my elder son and his wife were resident in Hong Kong, and so Nancy and I were regular visitors there. Chris invited us to dinner in the governor's mansion. Among the other guests was Jeremy Irons, who seemed to have forgiven, or at least forgotten, that I had chased him out of Balliol on the night of the state visit of the Chinese supremo. He was in a good mood, he told us, because he had spent the day in bed with the great actress Gong Li. Chris complained that Ted Heath regularly abused his hospitality, staying at the gubernatorial mansion while briefing against him to the Chinese government.

When Roy Jenkins died and the chancellorship became vacant, I, like others, thought of Chris as a possible successor. But I did not approach him because I believed at the time that he wished instead to become head of an Oxford college. Accordingly, I was the chief organizer of a campaign to elect Tom Bingham, as I will explain in a later chapter. When, later, Chris put his name forward, he swept the board. But he has never held it against me that I was leader of the opposition, and he was happy to be the guest of honour when Balliol gave me an eightieth birthday party in 2001.

# 13

## Three privy councillors

### Peter Brooke, Secretary of State for National Heritage

One of the acts of Mrs Thatcher's first government was to raise the fees of overseas students to a level which made Oxford more expensive than any Ivy League college in the USA. At Balliol, we were afraid this might destroy the international character on which we had long prided ourselves. I was instructed by the college to write to all its alumni in Parliament to protest against the policy. I received many letters of sympathy, but the longest and most helpful came from Peter Brooke, who was then MP for the cities of London and Westminster.

There was no hope, he told me, of persuading ministers to change their policy, but he agreed that Balliol's cosmopolitan membership was part of its essence. He suggested we should launch an appeal to alumni, and volunteered his services as a fundraiser. It was this that led to the inauguration of the Dervorguilla Appeal. In its early days Peter was a most helpful ally, until he became a minister of state in the Department of Education and Science and had to stand aside.

His appointment coincided in time with the successful run of the TV series, *Yes Minster*, starring Paul Eddington and Nigel Hawthorne, which featured the relationship between a minister and his permanent secretary. As it happened, the permanent secretary at the time was also a Balliol man, Sir David Hancock. Nancy and I organized a *Yes Minister* luncheon to which we decided to invite the two politicians and the two actors. (Sadly, Nigel Hawthorne was unable to attend.)

In 1984, Peter's son Jonathan came up to read PPE, and Peter would take whatever opportunity offered to visit Oxford and join his son in a game of cricket on the sports field. Jonathan was a keen athlete. He came to a reading party in the Alps in August in 1985, arriving in the midst of an unseasonable snowstorm.

Undeterred, he secured an athletic triumph. On special days during a reading party, one or other undergraduate used to run down the 4,000 feet to the village of Saint-Gervais to fetch up fresh croissants for breakfast in the chalet. Jonathan established a record of 45 minutes there and back, easily beating the previous record of 49 minutes.

At this period, Peter began a relationship with me that he had previously enjoyed with Russell Meiggs: each of us, should we find ourself in an out-of-the-way place, would send the other a postcard. As a result, there is now among my papers deposited in the British Library a fine collection of Peter Brooke autograph postcards in his exquisite handwriting.

From 1989 to 1992, Peter was Secretary of State for Northern Ireland and was often a guest speaker at British-Irish Association conferences. He gave up that office as a consequence of some minor gaffe during a television interview. He was succeeded by Sir Patrick Mayhew, who was kind enough to invite Nancy and me to stay with him in Hillsborough Castle outside Belfast. I took the opportunity to leave a copy of *The Road to Hillsborough* in the castle library.

In 1992, Peter moved to the Department of National Heritage. It was there that he made the greatest impact on my life. A year earlier, I had joined the board of the British Library under the chairmanship of Michael Saunders Watson, a landowner with a naval background. Peter now appointed me to replace him as chair. Michael regarded this as a shocking operation of the old-boy network, but he remained my good friend. Peter's real reason for appointing me, he told me, was that he wanted to show that the new library, now nearing completion, was not just a building site but an intellectual institution.

Friends who congratulated me on my appointment to the chair divided into two groups: some told me the job was a bed of nails, others that it was a can of worms. The construction of the new library at St Pancras had dragged on for many years, underfunded and way behind schedule. Supervision of the construction by the board of the library was a nightmare, since it was the Department of National Heritage, not the library board, that was the official client. If, when inspecting the site, we library people saw something going wrong – insulation, it might be, being put up upside down – we had no power to stop it. We could only send a message up through the echelons of the ministry, to come back down to the site long after the harm had been done. During my time as chair, though, we had one decisive piece of luck. John Major, then at the Treasury, for the first time set out a realistic budget and a realistic timescale. The new library building was completed only after I had ceased to be chair, but I was present when, in 1998, the Queen opened the new British Library. She commenced her speech with the words: 'This is an engagement that has been in my diary for a very long time.' For many years now I have visited St Pancras only as a reader, but I find the new library a delightful place to work, and am grateful to Peter for having allowed me a share in its creation.

## Boris Johnson, Foreign Secretary

The Balliol College Register for 1983 contains an entry which begins: 'JOHNSON Alexander Boris de Pfeffel: JOHNSON, Boris – b. 19 June 1964. New York. American. Generally known while at Balliol as Boris Johnson. Eton; Balliol 1983–7.' Boris came up to Balliol to read for the four-year course in classical literature, history and philosophy known as Literae Humaniores. Had he come up a few years earlier it would have been my job to teach him Plato and Aristotle. But by 1983 I was no longer a classics tutor, but Master of the college, and Boris' tutor in ancient philosophy was Jonathan Barnes, who went on record, in the first published biography of Boris, as regarding him as 'definitely a good egg'.

The head of a college supervises the education of undergraduates only at one remove. At Balliol at the end of each term the tutors assembled in the Master's dining room and the students were called in one after the other to listen to a report on their work. This ceremony was called 'handshaking', though no hands were shaken.

On the basis of the tutors' reports, I formed the judgement that while Boris had the necessary intelligence, he lacked the appropriate diligence to achieve the first-class degree that he clearly felt was his due.

Though he sat lightly to formal academic obligations, Boris did acquire a genuine love of the classics during his undergraduate years, and he was far from idle in social and political pursuits. In Balliol there was a debating club, the Arnold and Brackenbury Society. It was a light-hearted affair, resembling Matthew Arnold the frivolous undergraduate rather than Matthew Arnold the sage of sweetness and light. It was presided over by a stuffed owl named Mr Gladstone, and it had an absurdly complicated set of voting rules allowing, among other options, negative non-abstentions. Boris became president of this society, and on one occasion he and I spoke on the same side in favour of the motion, 'This house would prefer a double Napoleon to a pair of Wellingtons.' Our motion was carried overwhelmingly.

The Balliol JCR of those days was dominated by groups to the Left of the Communist Party, and Boris did not find it congenial. He spent more time with other clubs, such as the Bullingdon, and the Oxford Union. In 1986, he ran for the presidency of the Union. Though nothing like as rabid as the Balliol JCR, the Union was sufficiently left wing for it to be inconceivable for a Tory to be elected as president. Boris concealed his Conservative affiliation and let it be widely understood that he was a Social Democrat. So far as I know, he told no actual lies, but his strategy recalled Macaulay's words about the difference between lying and deceiving: 'Metternich told lies all the time, and never deceived any one; Talleyrand never told a lie and deceived the whole world.' With Talleyrand-like skill, Boris got himself elected as President of the Oxford Union in Trinity Term.

Shortly after this I was telephoned by an SDP MP, Dick Taverne, who told me that he was looking for an intern to work for him during the vacation. He inquired whether I could suggest any candidates. 'I've just the man for you', I said, 'bright and witty and with suitable political views. He's just finished being president of the Union, and his name is Boris Johnson.' When I summoned Boris to ask whether he was interested in the job, he burst out laughing: 'Master, don't you know I am a died-in-the-wool Tory?'

In 1987, Boris sat the final examinations. He was determined to get a first, and seemed confident that he could do so on the basis of six weeks of really hard work. Perhaps he might have been able to do so had he taken eight weeks: quite a few firsts have been gained on the basis of a last-minute spurt. But some weeks after the end of the examinations, Boris was summoned from France, told that his work was on the borderline between the first and second class, and instructed to appear for a viva, or oral examination.

A day or two later Boris knocked on my door, and presented a very humble appearance – the only time I have ever seen him do so. 'I am to be viva'd on Aristotle', he said. 'My tutor is in France – but I hear you know something about Aristotle. Would you be kind enough to give me a tutorial in preparation?' So we sat together for the best part of a day and went over a number of likely questions. In spite of this expert assistance, however, Boris achieved only an upper second. That is something that he has never forgotten. Nor has David Cameron, who got a first – not, in Lit. Hum. however, but in PPE, as Boris likes to remind people.

Boris has retained an affection for Balliol. He is married to Marina Wheeler, who was a college contemporary. He dedicated one of his books on the ancient world to his four classics tutors, and he has kept in touch with Jasper Griffin, who was his language tutor. While Boris was Mayor of London, Jasper assisted him from time to time with the classical passages with which he likes to decorate his speeches. At Boris' fiftieth birthday party, Jasper read out a Greek ode that he had composed in his honour.

In 2015, on the bicentenary of the Battle of Waterloo, I sent Boris a postcard reminding him that he had once eloquently expressed a preference for Napoleon over Wellington. 'Come referendum day', I said, 'remember your Europhile youth.' I received a witty, but non-committal reply. Later I wrote in serious terms:

Dear Boris

Last year I wrote you a frivolous letter on the subject of the referendum on Europe. I now write in all seriousness to ask you to throw your weight in favour of the UK remaining within the EU.

Having grown up during the years of the Second World War I have a sentimental attachment to the EU for having kept the peace between France and Germany for a longer period than any other since those two nations had an established identity. Intellectually I have no arguments in favour of the EU other than those that will be very familiar to you. But I am very impressed by the fact that the more intelligent and impartial portion of the press – the *FT* and *The Economist* for example – is strongly in favour of remaining, whereas the case for Brexit is pressed by the populist and xenophobe tabloids.

Among the Balliol friends and pupils with whom I am still in touch opinion is almost unanimous that leaving the EU would be a disaster not only for us but for other European nations. This has been expressed to me forcibly both by businessmen and diplomats. My Irish friends and students are particularly aghast at the prospect of Brexit.

I write to you now because at this moment you are in a remarkably influential position. Whatever happens at this week's summit, the PM is bound to say that he has achieved a great deal, and the Eurosceptics will say that it is not enough. You are one of the very few people whose personal decision could affect the outcome. You are respected by both parties to the debate, and you have kept your stance impartial between them both. Please use your influence in favour of a vote to remain.

Sadly, that letter remained unanswered. The outcome of the referendum, after Boris threw his weight behind Brexit, bore out the assertions in my final paragraph. But it did not achieve Boris' undisguised ambition to become prime minister: he was, as one newspaper put it, brought down by friendly fire. When I learned of his almost becoming prime minister I had vivid memories of the day when he almost got a first.

I last saw Boris in May 2017 at Jasper Griffin's eightieth birthday party. It was sporting of him to attend, in the middle of an election campaign. He read a witty poem he had written in honour of Jasper. But he was not welcomed by many of the guests, and some seriously considered walking out when he entered. As he left the college he was hissed and booed by members of the current undergraduate generation.

As he departed, I reflected ruefully on the college's part in his education. We had been privileged to be given the task of bringing up members of the nation's political elite. But what had we done for Boris? Had we taught him truthfulness? No. Had we taught him wisdom? No. What *had* we taught? Was it only how to make witty and brilliant speeches? I comforted myself with the thought that even Socrates was very doubtful whether virtue could be taught.

## Yvette Cooper, Privy Councillor

In an Oxford college it is always wise for the head of house and the president of the JCR to keep on good terms with each other. Even during the years of student revolution I was lucky to have a succession of presidents of personal charm. In the year 1969–70, the president was Martin Kettle, then a member of the Communist Party – that is to say, at the right-wing end of the JCR politics of those days. After a term in which the JCR had caused the dons a lot of trouble, Martin invited Nancy and me to let in the New Year of 1970, with him and other members of the JCR committee, in a cottage owned by his family in Great Langdale. It was a miniature replica of the Christmas truces in the 1914–18 trenches.

The last of my JCR presidents was Yvette Cooper, who came to the college in 1987. By this date, relations between senior and junior members were perfectly civil, but there remained points of conflict. During Yvette's term of office, the point of contention – which I remember only faintly – was whether senior or junior members had control of the JCR bar. It was on such issues that Yvette cut her political teeth.

My most vivid memories of the young Yvette, however, are not political. When the time came for me to leave the college she organized a gigantic farewell party for all the junior members. Her JCR committee baked an enormous goodbye cake for us, modelled as a replica of the college buildings. It was too large to fit through any door, but quickly vanished into the mouths of the junior members assembled in the quad.

Among the parting gifts Yvette gave me was a set of T-shirts. One of them, designed by Liza Dimbleby, portrays on its chest an elegant star-spangled nude. On the beach, I find it evokes a startled response from fellow holidaymakers: 'Wherever did you get that?', they ask. 'Oh', I used to say, during Gordon Brown's ministry, 'it was given to me by the Chief Secretary to the Treasury.'

Yvette and I see each other only rarely nowadays, at gaudies and the like. But when watching Parliament on television, I keep an eye open for her interventions from the back benches, which are always to the point. It is a sign of the current malaise of British politics that neither she nor her husband Ed Balls are able to contribute their talents to the highest levels of either government or opposition.

# 14

# Three heads of state

## King Olav V

It is the custom each year for the Norwegian nation to present the UK with a Christmas tree, set up in Trafalgar Square, as a thank-offering for the hospitality given to its royal family during the Second World War. King Olav V would make regular visits to London to set up the tree, and on several such occasions he travelled up to Balliol, where he had been an undergraduate in 1924. During his visit in 1979, my wife and I persuaded him to take luncheon in our family home, rather than in the Balliol SCR. He was wonderful with our young children, and answered their questions such as, 'Why aren't you wearing a crown?' and, 'What is your second name?' He told us that his cousin George VI, in preparation for his coronation, had to practise wearing the heavy crown for two hours a day two weeks beforehand. Nancy, having been brought up as a patriotic American to take a dim view of monarchs, wrote to her mother to describe how charming Olav was: 'He really is shy', she wrote, 'so you chatter away to set him at his ease, and then suddenly think "This is a *king*", and shut up. How grim, especially if you are shy, to have that effect on people.'

In the evening, the king took sherry with the undergraduates and dined with the fellows. Having been up very early in the morning he dozed off during the port, so I bundled him off to the lodgings for bed. In the night air in the quad he revived, decided it was too early for bed, and called for his pipe and his bowl. We got through quite a lot of Bell's before retiring about 1 a.m.

At midnight, the king's bodyguard entered in a state of alarm. A telephone call had been received saying, 'Balliol, you have the King of Norway: beware.' I persuaded the bodyguard that there was no real danger, and he did not need to sleep at the foot of the king's bed. King Olav agreed with me that the call was a hoax perpetrated by some practical joker at our neighbouring college: 'More like Trinity', he said, 'than the Lapland Liberation Front.'

A year later, while I was lecturing at Oslo University, King Olav returned our hospitality. He was clearly a popular monarch, and his subjects spoke with admiration of his skill and energy as a skier, in spite of his advanced age. I once took the opportunity to ask which was the part of his job that kept him busiest: 'I've all those things to sign', he said with a sigh. So Christopher Robin's Alice was right after all.

In 1981, the oil company BP, who enjoyed substantial revenue from Norwegian oilfields, offered to pay for a portrait of the king, by an artist of his choice, to hang in Balliol Hall. King Olav came to unveil it. The college bursar, worried lest someone might paint a false moustache on it, slept with it in his room until the day of the ceremony. But all passed off well, and one hundred undergraduates in collars and ties stood respectfully silent while the portrait was unveiled. Sadly, the portrait itself was a disappointment, closely resembling the postcards of the king that one could buy in any Norwegian airport.

When I was fundraising, I wrote to Balliol alumni to invite them to present items for an auction to be held at Christie's for the college's benefit. King Olav, at a luncheon I gave in London in honour of his eightieth birthday, presented me with a gold watch given him by his grandfather, King Edward VII. Embarrassingly, when the auction catalogue was drawn up, the watch, because it bore no English hallmark, was described as being 'of yellow metal'.

We had luncheon again with King Olav on my next lecture visit to Oslo in 1987. He was now eighty-six, and losing his sight, but it was the unseasonably warm weather, not his infirmity, which kept him from skiing. In the following April he paid a state visit to Britain, and we were invited to the state dinner in the banqueting hall at Windsor. That was the last time we saw him – it was also the last occasion the banqueting hall was used before being set on fire while the castle was being rewired.

## Francesco Cossiga

When Italian statesmen were honoured by Oxford, I was often placed beside them at luncheon because there was a shortage of dons who spoke Italian. The first Italian president I met in this way was Pertini. It was at the Encaenia at which Margaret Thatcher would have received her honorary degree, had it been approved by Congregation. Pertini, a lifelong socialist, had been chosen to be honoured beside her so that political balance should be kept. He lamented her absence: 'Si chiama donna di ferro', he said, 'ma dentro quell petto batte un cuor dolce e gentile.'*

The Italian president I did get to know was Francesco Cossiga. When we first met, all I knew of him was that he had been prime minister at the time of the murder of Aldo Moro, and had since become head of state. We had in common an interest in the writings of Thomas More and John Henry Newman. As an admirer of Newman, Cossiga liked to spend time at Oriel, Newman's college, which made him an honorary fellow. But he also enjoyed visiting Balliol, aware of its important, if ambiguous, role in the Oxford Movement.

During a visit to our lodgings in 1986, he noticed a large group of students in the quad bearing a banner. 'A very peaceful demonstration', he said, 'but what Italian policy are they protesting?' I explained that the issue was a purely local grievance; we had recently reduced the number of hours when the front gate was open at night, and the banner bore the words 'Keep Balliol open'.

When Roy Jenkins became chancellor, he gave Cossiga and myself honorary degrees on the same day, and we were placed beside each other in the procession. This was the beginning of a friendship that lasted for the rest of his life: we would meet sometimes in Oxford, sometimes in London, and sometimes in the Quirinal Palace in Rome. When Nancy and I entertained him in our own home, the King's Mound, he wrote a gracious thank-you letter comparing his

---

* 'She's called the Iron Lady, but inside that breast beats a sweet and kind heart.'

visit to the visit of Erasmus to Thomas More's house in Chelsea. I was flattered: not so my wife, remembering Erasmus' description of Dame Alice as 'neither a pearl nor a girl.' One of Cossiga's last acts was to persuade the pope to make St Thomas More the patron saint of politicians. He sent me a copy of the dossier he had drawn up to make the case for choosing More for the role.

Though Cossiga and I became friendly, there was always the difference between us that I was an agnostic and he remained a devout Catholic. One day he surprised me by going into Blackwell's, the main academic bookstore in Oxford, and telling the manager to send a copy of each of my books (some thirty-odd by then) to Cardinal Martini of Milan. I received, some weeks later, a courteous but puzzled letter of thanks from the cardinal. Cossiga's action baffled me no less than him. Only later did an Italian friend offer me a plausible explanation: Cossiga, a conservative Catholic, was unhappy with Martini's liberal tendencies, though he did not live to read the cardinal's posthumous critique of current Vatican policies. Cossiga was also known to enjoy playing practical jokes. Perhaps his purpose in burdening the cardinal with my collected works was to warn him: 'If you pursue your liberal line you will end up by believing no more than an agnostic like Anthony Kenny.'

In the last telephone conversation we had, shortly before his death, Cossiga asked me, 'Can you tell me why the Conservative Party has fired its leader, the Catholic Ian Duncan Smith, and replaced him with a Jew, Michael Howard?' This brought home to me how closely intertwined in Italy are politics and religion. No English politician would have seen the switch of leadership in such confessional terms; and indeed, until that moment, I had not even known that Ian Duncan Smith was a Catholic.

## Bill Clinton

I had an impact on Bill Clinton's life long before he made any impression on mine. In 1967 he won a Rhodes Scholarship to Oxford, and placed Balliol first on his list of choices of colleges.

He wanted to read for a second degree in PPE there, but we tutors in the subject, having examined his papers, passed him on to his college of second choice. When, years later, he was President of the USA, and I was writing a memoir of my time at Balliol, I wrote to him to ask if he minded my telling the story of his rejection. By return of post came a postcard giving permission – on condition that I pointed out that he had been so happy at University College in 1968–70 that, with hindsight, he was glad to have been found wanting at Balliol.

The presidential campaign of Governor Clinton caused much excitement among Rhodes Scholars, past and present. The Rhodes House staff also became involved, to a surprising and unwelcome extent. This was because journalists and others unfriendly to the campaign would telephone, and sometimes visit, Rhodes House in pursuit of imaginary material to support various calumnies about Clinton's Oxford days. Things became so difficult that I had to remove the Clinton file from the office to my bedroom. We were, in the end, able to convince all parties that it was not proper for us to release material from any Rhodes Scholar dossier without the permission of the Scholar in question, and of the authors of confidential reports. This policy, though surely the only defensible one, had the disadvantage that one had to see circulating in the newspapers false allegations that could have been refuted by producing material from our Clinton file. Fortunately, most of the absurd stories collapsed under their own weight in the run-up to polling day.

On election night, once Ohio had declared for Clinton, the result was assured and I retired to bed. My wife, as a loyal citizen of America, stayed up to hear the president elect's acceptance speech at 4 a.m. GMT. We had recovered sufficiently the next day to send out invitations to all current US Scholars to a champagne reception. At the party we toasted not only the first, but also the second, Rhodes Scholar president. Who knows: he or she might well be present in the room. A package of congratulations, accompanied with advice, was signed by all the Scholars and despatched to Little Rock, Arkansas.

In June 1993, there was a North American Rhodes Reunion, and President Clinton attended a party at the British Embassy. It was on that occasion that I first met him and experienced at first hand his legendary charm. Commonly, when you are introduced to a grand person, the grand person, for most of the time he or she is talking to you, is looking over your shoulder to see if there is someone more important nearby. Not so with Bill Clinton: he talks to you as if you were the only person in the whole room whom he wanted to meet.

In that year, it turned out, he was not the only Rhodes Scholar to serve as head of state. The secretary of the trust in Pakistan, Wasim Sajjad (Wadham 1964), was the chair of the senate. On the resignation of the then President of Pakistan he took over the presidential duties during the period leading up to the elections. It was an odd experience to have even an acting head of state on one's payroll.

In the following year, President Clinton visited Oxford to receive a degree by diploma, and part of his programme was a visit to Rhodes House. At one time, some 16 members of the White House security and protocol staff had 24-hour passes giving them access to the house. Massive telephone cables were swung through the balcony windows on the top floor, and electronic searching devices were installed in the garden. The upstairs sitting room was converted to a 'holding room' for the First Lady. Security helicopters droned incessantly overhead. White House plans for the event changed daily, and the vice chancellor's secretary took to printing 'Ninth Draft', or whatever, in large letters at the head of her communications.

My son Charles, who was living with us at the time, found it difficult to get into his own home. When challenged, he replied, 'If the key I have in my hand opens this door, will you believe I live here?' On another occasion, when held up by security, he told them that he was the son of the Warden. 'Can you prove it?', said the guard – a query that gave great offence to my wife.

The eventual visit to Rhodes House took place immediately after the president had received his degree from the chancellor. The Rhodes trustees, who had attended the ceremony in the Sheldonian Theatre, sprinted up Parks Road to assemble, ahead of the motorcade, to welcome the president at the entrance to Rhodes House. When the presidential car arrived, the first person to get out was not the president, but another man of the same build, wearing the same clothes, and with the same haircut. He was presumably a decoy who would have been the victim if an assassin had been waiting to get the president in his sights. I hope he was well paid.

When Mrs Clinton appeared – preceded likewise by a doppel-ganger – it turned out that she was wearing a suit of exactly the same shade and material as my wife. They both looked slightly sheepish as my wife escorted her up to the holding room. Three different sections of White House staff had taken the responsibility for providing tea for the ladies: their instructions had contradicted each other with the upshot that no tea appeared, and our own staff had to improvise. Meanwhile, I took the president into Milner Hall to take tea with the Rhodes Scholars. In welcoming him at the microphone, I was able to present him with a classified document which we had zealously protected during his election campaign. This was the tutors' reports of his first two terms as a Scholar. The president had never seen these before. He gave a very passing imitation of a person dreading what he was about to hear, but his expression turned from apprehension to relief as he listened to me reading them out. They were generally positive, praising his keenness and intelligence. However, they called for further reading to be done. Clinton clearly took to heart this advice of long ago, because immediately after leaving Rhodes House he went off to Blackwell's bookstore.

Clinton retained a warm affection for Sir Edgar 'Bill' Williams, who had been Warden at the time of his Rhodes Scholarship. Williams was not an unqualified admirer of the president: he once said to me, 'If we have to have a Rhodes Scholar president, why does it have to be Bill Clinton of all people?' But they must have been on good terms all those years ago. On the occasion of Williams' eightieth birthday, we gave him a party in Rhodes House: he was called away to the telephone to discover that Clinton was calling from the White House to give his birthday greetings in person.

Since leaving Rhodes House, I have not had any further conversations with Clinton, but occasionally have heard him lecture. He is one of the best lecturers I have known, able to vary effortlessly tone and topic. He begins with a flat, fluent, noteless, tour d'horizon, makes a few witty jokes, and then moves into political advocacy, ending up with the ardour of a preacher.

In 2003, my successor at Rhodes House organized a spectacular event to mark the centenary of Cecil Rhodes' death. My wife and I attended a ceremony in Westminster Hall, presided over by a remarkable trio: Nelson Mandela, Bill Clinton and Tony Blair. Of the three grandees, it was Clinton who made the best speech:

> At this time when our peoples are worried about the future of the modern world, it is symbolic of all the progress we have made that all these politicians feel safe in this room where Sir Thomas More and Charles I were tried and found wanting. They lost their heads, and here are we looking forward to the reception afterwards.

# 15

## Three judges

### Jim Kilbrandon, Lord of Appeal

Every Oxford college has a 'Visitor'. Traditionally, the Visitor provides the ultimate tribunal of appeal on matters of contention between the students and the fellows, and between the fellows and the head of house. Recent legislation has trimmed the powers of Visitors, but they were in full force when I joined Balliol. Most colleges have Visitors appointed by statute: the Visitor of Merton is the Archbishop of Canterbury, and that of Oriel is the Queen. Unusually, Balliol has the right to elect its own Visitor. In 1974 we elected Lord Kilbrandon.

As Jim Shaw, Kilbrandon had read PPE at Balliol in the 1920s and been called to the Scottish Bar in 1932, rising to the most senior post in that profession in 1957. When chosen as Visitor, he had been for three years a Lord of Appeal and a member of the House of Lords. He had made a national reputation as chair of the Royal Commission on the Constitution, which laid the foundations for eventual devolved government in Scotland.

Because of the Visitor's role in conflict resolution, it has often been said, 'Happy is the college that has no visitations.' That was the case during Jim's 12-year tenure of office. His official functions turned out to be entirely ceremonial. For instance, when I was pre-elected as Master in April 1978 by the fellows assembled in the college chapel, Kilbrandon waited in the lodgings for the senior fellow to present me to him, along with the official documents of my appointment. I made a declaration of fidelity and he swore me in.

Though never called on to arbitrate, Jim was a frequent and popular Visitor, a familiar figure because of his great height and the limp he had acquired through a skiing accident when on active service. From time to time, Jim's stay in the lodgings would coincide with that of Harold Macmillan, but he kept more regular hours than the older man. One evening he retired to bed shortly after midnight, leaving me to gossip with the chancellor into the small hours. 'That's the problem with judges', said Macmillan. 'No stamina any more.'

My serious cooperation with Jim was triggered by the New Ireland Forum, launched by the Irish leader Garret FitzGerald, which published its report in 1984. This spelt out a number of proposals for moves towards the reconciliation of Ulster Unionism and Irish nationalism. The report was initially dismissed by the British government. The British-Irish Association, however, thought that it deserved a more thought-out response, and commissioned an independent inquiry to examine the merits of the Forum proposals. Because of the prestige of his report on Scottish devolution, it was Jim Kilbrandon who was asked to chair the inquiry. He assembled an all-party group, including David Howell, a Tory ex-cabinet minister, and Alf Dubs, later a Labour peer, plus a handful of other politicians, academics and business people. Jim asked me to join the committee and act as vice chair.

Serving on the committee involved a number of fascinating contacts with politicians in Northern Ireland and the Republic, which I will describe in a later chapter. Meetings of the inquiry commonly took place in Balliol and, because Jim's health had begun to fail, much of the work of chairing meetings and preparing papers fell to me. It became clear that we were not going to achieve a unanimous report: eight of us were willing to explore the idea of joint Anglo-Irish authority in Northern Ireland; a number of others were afraid of a Unionist backlash. Jim was on the side of the majority: he kept saying that it was just common sense. But the rest of us felt that the common sense of an Episcopalian Scotsman might not be the same as that of a Presbyterian Unionist.

In the end, the Kilbrandon Report was in two parts: one unanimous and the other divided. The unanimous part recommended a number of specific reforms, including a Bill of Rights to protect minorities, with a role for the Irish Republic in its enforcement. The minority report suggested only minor tinkering with the status quo. The report of the majority, to which Jim and I belonged, favoured what we called 'Cooperative Devolution'. This included a much strengthened police authority to consist of a minister from the Northern Ireland Office, the Minister of Justice from the Republic, and three Northern Ireland members, two from the Protestant majority, and one from the Catholic minority. The top tier of government, we urged, should be a five-man executive similarly constructed.

When the Kilbrandon Report was debated in the Northern Ireland Assembly, it was dismissed by Unionists as 'fantasy and green dreams'. At a press conference about the New Ireland Forum a few days later, Mrs Thatcher dismissed the Forum's three proposals. 'A unified Ireland', she said, 'was one solution that is out. A second solution was a confederation of two states. That is out. A third solution was joint authority. That is out.' Behind the scenes, however, steps were being taken that led, first of all to the Hillsborough Agreement of November 1985, and later the Good Friday Agreement of 1998, which took the involvement of the Republic in the affairs of Northern Ireland to a degree far beyond the 'green dreams' of the Kilbrandon Report. It remains to be seen whether the peace process, in which Jim and I had a tiny initial part, will be brought to a halt, or go into reverse, as a result of recent developments such as Brexit.

## Tom Bingham, Senior Law Lord

I knew quite a bit about Tom Bingham before I met him, because he was something of a Balliol legend. As an undergraduate he had been elected president of the JCR, defeating by one vote Paul Sarbanes, the future Maryland senator. Once elected, Tom had been involved with a group of contemporaries who had taken supplies to Hungary at the time of the Russian invasion. My friend Maurice Keen had many a story to tell of him. The two of them had been friends ever since they had done national service together in the Royal Ulster Rifles. They had gone on to read history together at Balliol, where they spent vacations together. They had paid a visit to Sligger's chalet, where Tom, unlike Maurice, had taken a liking to the Alps and had climbed Mont Blanc. Tom, on leaving the college, had then spent a summer in America as a Coolidge Pathfinder.

In spite of not having a law degree, Tom was called to the Bar in 1959 and quickly acquired a reputation in the commercial courts. He caught the eye of the general public when he was appointed by David Owen to conduct an inquiry into the supply of oil to Rhodesia during the period of UN sanctions. His report, critical of Harold Wilson's government, was regarded as a model of historical research and judicious comment.

It was indeed African affairs that brought Tom and me together. One of the first papers to arrive on my desk when I became Master was a well-informed and well-presented report on foreign investment and apartheid, prepared by a JCR working party. The paper argued that we should cease to hold shares in any companies active in South Africa. Some fellows, on the other hand, including a succession of bursars, felt strongly that it was wrong for an educational institution to allow ethical or political considerations to affect the choice of investments. I tried to devise a scheme that would allow us to operate a 'clean hands' portfolio while fulfilling our responsibility for the prudent management of our trust funds.

The college agreed that we should become active shareholders, monitoring, and if necessary challenging, the South African activities of the companies in whom we held shares. We set up a Shareholder Action Committee, with four members of governing body, two junior members and two alumni members. With Michael Posner, Tom Bingham agreed to accept appointment as an alumnus member, and generously gave his time, authority and experience to the work of the committee. Unlike my experience of some other joint committees, we found the contribution of the undergraduate members valuable, and one of them, after graduation, founded an ethical investment fund which prospered.

In 1980, at the young age of 46, Tom was made a judge of the Queen's Bench Division. He continued to offer help and advice to the college. From time to time, right-wing newspapers would publish false accounts of the communist past of my predecessor

Christopher Hill. As some of the calumnies reflected on the college as well as on Christopher, I asked Tom whether it would be appropriate for us to fund Christopher in a libel action. His advice was firmly against doing so. No doubt Christopher would win the case, but in the course of the trial it was likely that unrelated embarrassments might occur. Tom also helped me with my involvement in Irish affairs, writing a paper, in connection with proposals for joint authority, on the flexibility of the concept of sovereignty. During the Brexit debate I wished that I had kept a copy of it.

In 1986, Jim Kilbrandon retired as Visitor, and the fellows were unanimous in wishing to elect Tom as his successor. Their admiration of Bingham was shared by Chancellor Macmillan when I consulted him, and one of his last appearances was at the Balliol Society dinner at which Jim handed over the visitorship to Tom. The Lord Chancellor of the time showed that he shared our high opinion of Tom by making him a Lord Justice of Appeal in the same year.

I have neither the space nor the competence to comment on Lord Bingham's effect on English law during his years first as Master of the Rolls, then as Lord Chief Justice, and finally as Senior Law Lord. Fifty lawyers from many countries did so in a magnificent liber amicorum, *Tom Bingham and the Transformation of the Law*, published in 2009 on his retirement from the judicial House of Lords.

When Roy Jenkins died in 2003, I suggested to Tom that he should put his hat in the ring to succeed him as Chancellor of Oxford University. He agreed to do so, and threw himself into the campaign with remarkable gusto. I had many lively meetings with him and his wife, his sons Harry and Kit, and his daughter Kate, constructing a manifesto and drawing up lists of potential nominators and supporters. We happily walked round with badges saying, 'I'm a Binghamist'. As in the previous election, the contest was essentially between two Balliol men, this time Bingham and Patten. But I was not aware of any of the embarrassment, and sometimes animosity, that had disfigured the earlier contest. I was sorry, but not downcast, that my candidate did not win the election. Tom would have made an excellent chancellor, but Chris has done the job magnificently and he has the unquestioned advantage of being still alive.

Of all the people I have known, Tom Bingham is the one for whom I have the greatest admiration, both intellectually and morally. He was a delightful conversationalist and a witty after-dinner speaker, but underneath the urbanity there was always deep seriousness. He was forever anxious to attain the precise truth about any factual issue, and to balance justly the arguments for or against any proposal.

Two of Tom's remarks stay in my mind. One, made in the course of a controversy I have now forgotten, was: 'In all the years of her reign, the Queen has never once put a constitutional foot wrong.' The other was made at a party when I was teasing Cormac Murphy-O'Connor for receiving Tony Blair into the Catholic Church. I said that Blair should at least have been given a long period of penance, such as that which St Ambrose had imposed on the Emperor Theodosius, who had been responsible for a massacre. 'Oh yes', Cormac said, shaking his head, 'the invasion of Iraq was a mistake – a terrible mistake.' Tom, who was in the same conversational circle, interjected: 'No, your eminence: it was a wicked act – a very wicked act.'

## Laurie Ackermann, judge of the Constitutional Court of South Africa

When I became secretary of the Rhodes Trust in 1989 I inherited a set of overseas secretaries, each responsible for the selection procedures in one of the countries which sent Rhodes Scholars to Oxford. They were all remarkable people, but the most remarkable of all was Laurie Ackermann, the South African secretary. Laurie was a descendant of an Afrikaans family, some of whose members had been interned in concentration camps during the Anglo-Boer War. He had read law in Afrikaans at the University of Stellenbosch from 1951 to 1954, and then in English as a Rhodes Scholar at Worcester College, Oxford, from 1954 to 1956. When I got to know him he spoke and wrote faultless, and indeed elegant, English, but Afrikaans remained the language used at home.

In 1958, he began to practise at the Pretoria Bar. In the same year he married Denise du Toit, who was to become an internationally renowned feminist theologian. Laurie rose rapidly and was appointed a Supreme Court judge in 1980. South Africa was still in thrall to the apartheid system, and in 1987 there came a day when Laurie had to hand out a verdict on a member of the ANC. Recalling that day, he told me that there was no doubt that on the evidence before the court the accused was guilty as charged, and he had no alternative but to impose the death penalty. But at some point, he felt, a judge must ask himself about the morality of the system of justice that he was administering. This should not affect a decision in a particular case, but it should affect the judge's assessment of his own role. On that basis he resigned from the bench, giving up his salary, his pension and many of his friends.

For a while Laurie was out of a job, but H. E. Oppenheimer came to the rescue, founding a chair of Human Rights Law at the University of Stellenbosch, of which Laurie was appointed the first holder. During the last years of apartheid he was also occasionally employed in a judicial capacity in the supreme courts of what were then known as 'the front-line states' of Lesotho and Namibia. On our first visit to the Rhodes community in South Africa, Nancy and I stayed with the Ackermanns in their house in Rondebosch near the Boschendal botanic park with its incredible variety of wild flowers. Thus began a warm friendship that lasts to this day, though problems of health and age mean that we see each other only rarely.

During my time as Secretary of the Rhodes Trust, Laurie displayed the most extraordinary humility in his relations with me. He was professionally and morally my superior, but he always obeyed unquestioningly any instructions that I gave him on behalf of the trustees. In Cecil Rhodes' will, scholarships were assigned to four named Cape schools which, up till the time when Laurie took up the national secretaryship, had never opened their doors to black people or women. The worldwide Rhodes community regarded the continued existence of these scholarships as a scandal, and in 1988 the Rhodes trustees commenced legal proceedings for their abolition. Discussions and negotiations with the schools continued over several years, and throughout Laurie loyally supported the trustees' position.

South Africa, however, was beginning to change, faster than anyone had expected. F. W. de Klerk began to dismantle apartheid legislation, and a new law permitted schools to open their doors to all races. The named schools did so, and thus undercut the case presented to the court by the trustees, who accordingly in 1991 withdrew their application for abolition. After the release of Nelson Mandela, Laurie took part in framing a new constitution for South Africa and became one of the first members of its Constitutional Court. Already, in the 1980s, he had joined in talks with exiled ANC leaders, and his principled stand in the dark days of apartheid naturally made him a hero of the new South Africa.

As National Secretary of the Rhodes Trust he presided over each year's selection of South African Rhodes Scholars, and ensured a regular supply of first-rate candidates. Among many of them, I recall in particular two that came up in 1991: Fanie du Toit and Chris Landsberg – one an Afrikaner, the other black. The two were inseparable, and symbolized for us the best of the post-apartheid era. If any Rhodes Scholar in residence took issue with any decision of Rhodes House, Laurie would disentangle the problem with impeccable courtesy to both sides.

Each year, Nancy and I hosted the assembled national Rhodes secretaries in Rhodes House, and the Ackermanns were faithful attenders. In July 1990, they joined a group of Scholars for a reading party on bioethics at the Saint-Gervais chalet. In later years, Kennys and Ackermanns took holidays together, most memorably a visit to Namaqualand in order to catch the two weeks of the year when what is normally a desert is covered with a counterpane of wild flowers of every colour. In 2006, I spent several weeks as a visiting professor at Stellenbosch, and we relied on the Ackermanns to explain to us the functioning of the new South Africa. They took us to visit

Robben Island; when we returned to the mainland we found that the hubcaps of Laurie's car had been 'liberated'. Laurie was stoical. Given the choice between an unjust system, a civil war and a crime wave, he said, the last of the three was the best option.

Despite being married to a celebrated theologian, Laurie, in the years I spent time with him, was not at all religious. He favoured an upright secular morality, inspired largely by the thought of Kant, about whom he wrote a book in retirement. But his morality was not at all austere. He was an authority on wine, and could identify by taste not only the vineyard but the year of a fine claret. He had a dry sense of humour and would tell jokes without moving his normally solemn features – until, at the moment you saw the point, his face would crumple into delighted laughter. I wish we were not separated by the length of two continents.

# 16

## Three dissidents

### Ivan Supek, Croatian dissident

Ivan Supek, a philosopher who became Rector of Zagreb University in the 1960s, was an ambitious man. Among other things he was a dramatist, and he wrote a play about Marcantonio de Dominis, a colourful figure of the Counter-Reformation. De Dominis was a Roman Catholic bishop of Spalato, but he was anxious to bring together the different branches of Christianity, becoming an archimandrite in the Greek Orthodox Church, and later Dean of Windsor in the Church of England. On his return to Europe, he predictably fell foul of the Roman Inquisition and ended his days in prison. Supek saw de Dominis' character as a model, and wished to play a role in the twentieth century similar to that which the archbishop had played in the seventeenth. He saw himself as a peacemaker between Croats and Serbs in Yugoslavia, and between East and West during the Cold War.

Accordingly, he set up in Dubrovnik an inter-university centre where faculty members from both parts of Yugoslavia, and from either side of the Iron Curtain, were invited for periods of two weeks to lecture to groups of students similarly constituted. The students would stay for a full term, receiving lectures from a succession of visiting faculty members. In the winter of 1975 I was invited, with Philippa Foot and a dozen other philosophers from America and Scandinavia, to be a 'resource person' for the first part of the term. I lectured on history and ethics and found it exhilarating to address such a variety of students from different political systems – though they all had in common, fortunately for us, a knowledge of English. We never learned the surnames of most of them: they would be known, in medieval style, as Thomas of Heidelberg, or Pyotr of Kiev, and so on. Supek was a genial and visionary presiding presence.

Though our courses offered no problems, Philippa and I arrived in Yugoslavia at a dramatic moment. The beginning of our stay coincided with a conference arranged by the international Pugwash group – a group of physicists who commonly met in Nova Scotia to share concerns about nuclear weapons. That year the group had decided to broaden its horizons and hold a general symposium on science and ethics in Dubrovnik. Along with others, Philippa and I were invited to read papers to the conference. Among those also invited were eight philosophers from Belgrade, known as the Praxis School. These were critical and open-minded Marxists, who had been in good standing with the League of Communists until 1968, when they were alleged to have instigated student demonstrations. President Tito had tried to get them removed from their posts, but they were manfully defended by their colleagues, who had considerable powers under the self-management laws then governing Belgrade University. In 1974, however, the laws were changed to give more power to the external members of the university council. This was widely seen as a prelude to the dismissal, and possibly the imprisonment, of the Praxis members.

The Pugwash Conference presented an excellent opportunity for an international protest against the harassment of the Praxis School. Philippa and I prepared a document to circulate to conference members if it should turn out that the Belgrade philosophers had been imprisoned or prevented from attending. By the time we set out for Dubrovnik, it was still uncertain what had happened to our colleagues in Belgrade, so we carried in our suitcases cyclostyled copies of the protest for distribution. But though we were nervous as we passed through customs, nobody searched our luggage, and when we emerged we were met by a welcome party headed by none other than Mihailo Marković, the head of the School. The cyclostyled protests became scrap paper.

## Mihailo Marković, Serbian dissident

Shortly after Philippa and I took our leave of the Praxis philosophers they were suspended under the new law. Through the good offices of

Sir Alexander Glen, a Balliol man who had been with Tito's Partisans during the war, I made a full protest to the Yugoslav ambassador in London. We were not able to get the suspension revoked, but we managed to achieve comparatively humane terms. Though the eight were forbidden to teach or take part in university government, they continued to be paid a salary and were allowed to write and travel.

Under this regime, Mihailo was able to accept a visiting professorship in Pennsylvania. On his way thither he paid a visit to Oxford, where he stayed in our house. He was a delightful guest, talking philosophy with me, singing with Nancy and playing chess with my seven-year-old son Robert.

These happy memories were swept away when Yugoslavia broke up in the 1990s. Slobodan Milosevic rose to be head of the Serbian Communists and began destabilizing Croatia, which declared independence in July 1991. Marković rose to be vice president of the Serbian Socialist Party, and became a guru and propagandist for Milosevic. He helped organize plans for a new Yugoslavia that would, in effect, be a greater Serbia, with the Muslims of Bosnia encircled and enfeebled, in an enclave resembling the South African Bantustans.

In the course of the conflict between Serbia and Croatia, Dubrovnik became a centre of battle, cut off from the rest of the country and under a state of siege. Kathy Wilkes of St Hilda's, who had been, like Philippa and myself, a resource person at Supek's institute, stayed at her post there during most of the siege of 1991, and risked her life several times driving a lorry from Britain into the city with essential supplies. She was later awarded the Freedom of the City.

I saw Marković only once after the end of the war, at an international philosophy conference. I had been unsure whether I should speak to him at all, but when in advance I asked a Croatian friend for her opinion she said, 'Of course you must.' We had a polite, but stilted, conversation. Other philosophers seemed to have received different advice, because Mihailo spent most of the conference standing alone.

# Julius Tomin, Czech dissident

In 1979, Oxford philosophers received a letter from Dr Julius Tomin, inviting them to visit an unofficial seminar that he conducted in his apartment in Prague. Tomin, we discovered, had received a doctorate in philosophy in the Charles University under the widely respected Jan Patočka. After the Soviet intervention put an end to the Prague Spring, he held a visiting professorship at the University of Hawaii, but rather than accept a permanent post there he returned to Czechoslovakia. He and his wife were signatories of Charter 77, a manifesto pressing for the implementation of human rights guarantees. As such, they were regularly harassed by the police.

Unable to get an academic job, Julius organized informal courses in philosophy in his apartment for young people who were denied access to university because their parents were dissidents. The seminar met every Wednesday between October and June. The Oxford philosophy sub-faculty made grants for its members to lecture to the seminars, and its secretary, Kathy Wilkes, made arrangements for philosophers from London, Norway, Canada, West Germany and Australia to pay visits. The visits continued until March 1980, without problems: lecturers gave their papers, discussed them with Tomin's students, and left the country in the normal way.

In March, Bill Newton-Smith, the senior tutor of Balliol, was reading a paper on the philosophy of science when the seminar was broken up by 14 policemen. He was then interrogated for two and a half hours, and told to tell his colleagues that no one must contact Tomin, who was 'an enemy of the state'. He was then deported to West Germany in the middle of the night.

As the head of Newton-Smith's college, I sent a letter of protest to the Czech Embassy in London, and followed it up with an interview with the minister, Dr Telicka. I pressed him to state in what way Bill's activities had been illegal, and under what law and in what respects Tomin and his associates were regarded as an illegal society. I also asked him to send me a copy of the relevant law as I had a particular interest in getting clear about the legal situation because, under arrangements made much earlier, it was my turn to be the next visiting lecturer.

I felt it would be hardly decent to call off the lecture, and continued preparation for the visit. Meanwhile, in Prague, Tomin was taken off for interrogation and held for 48 hours. Nancy and I were due to arrive less than a day after his release, and as we flew across Europe we wondered whether we would be turned back on arrival. The Czech authorities must have known of my visit since my name had been published in an English communist newspaper that was read in Prague. But we encountered no problems at immigration, and were met by Julius' wife, Zdena, who gave us a quick tour of Prague – just in case we were unable to make use of the package tour we had purchased for the days after the seminar. Over a snack of Moravian ham and Pilsner beer we gave messages to the Tomins from friends in Oxford, and passed over money due to Julius as payment for an article in the *New Statesman*.

When we arrived in the Tomins' flat we were relieved to see that there were no policemen camped on the staircase, as there had been on recent occasions. I met Julius for the first time ten minutes before the seminar was due to start: he did not want to discuss his recent arrests, but was anxious to get clear about the meaning of some passages in Aristotle's *Ethics*. The topic of my lecture was Aristotle's conception of the good life, which differed in his two principal treatises: in the *Nicomachean Ethics* the ideal life for a human being is the life of a philosopher; in the *Eudemian Ethics*, philosophy – though very important – is no more than a part of the good life. I intended to argue that the Eudemian claim was the more realistic.

I started to lecture, and Tomin translated into Czech the Aristotelian passages and my commentary on them. We reached a passage where Aristotle argues that philosophy is the best of all lives because it is the hardest to take away: you can pursue it, even if you lose your money and your friends. This passage was heavily scored in Julius' copy of the text. At that moment, a watcher in the window corner said, 'They're here', and 20 uniformed and plain clothes policemen filed into the apartment. My wife and I were escorted by the police to their headquarters in Bartolomějská Street. The Czech members of the seminar were made to follow, and were held in the same building for three hours before being taken to detention centres. Tomin used the time to give his students a further lecture on Aristotle.

Nancy and I were separated and interrogated by two different groups of detectives. They insisted that it was illegal to talk to Tomin's group, while being unwilling to specify what law had been broken.

'Who sent you to Prague?'

'No one *sent* me.'

'What was the content of your lecture?'

That was an easy one, and I bored them for several minutes on the topic of the Aristotelian manuscript tradition. From time to time I inquired whether I was under arrest, and asked them to contact the British Embassy, but they claimed to be having trouble with the telephone.

Eventually the police drove me to my hotel and made me pack our luggage under their watchful eyes. They pointed out, helpfully, that when clearing the drawers I had missed two of Nancy's skirts. We went to reception and they collected our passports from the hotel manager. 'Why do you want them?', I asked, 'I'm in your custody anyway.' 'They will be returned to you at the frontier.' That was very cheering: it meant that we were not going to be held indefinitely, but simply deported. I was taken to the police waiting room and reunited with Nancy.

At three o'clock in the morning a police limousine picked us up and drove us the 200 kilometres to the border with West Germany. The driver handed our passports to the frontier guard, who stamped them to the effect that our visas had been terminated because we were in violation of Article 202 of the penal code – which forbade hooliganism. It took us some time, at seven o'clock in the morning, to convince the German frontier officials that we were not drug smugglers, and that the piece of hooliganism for which I had been expelled was lecturing on Aristotle. But once convinced, they were most helpful and sped us quickly home.

The Czech members of the seminar were held for 48 hours and then released without any charges being made. Some weeks after our expulsion, Kathy Wilkes became the third Oxford don to be deported, after giving an impromptu lecture to 15 of Tomin's students while sheltering from the rain in a cave on a country walk.

Later in 1980, Julius and his wife and children left Prague on a five-year visa. In 1979, Balliol had invited him to give a brief series of endowed lectures. At that time, he had declined on the grounds that it would be unlikely he would be allowed back into Czechoslovakia. I was therefore surprised when I learned of his decision to come in September, but both Balliol and King's College Cambridge welcomed him as a guest, providing hospitality and a stipend in addition to the lecture fee.

However, some remarks of his in England about a Polish workers' strike were taken as provocative by the Czech authorities. His citizenship was revoked, and he could not return home. I tried hard to get it restored, using the good offices of prominent British figures who had influence with Husák's government. That government offered to restore it on certain conditions which Tomin was unwilling to accept. Those of us responsible for inviting him accepted that it was our duty to fund him until he became self-supporting. A group of us subscribed anonymously to a fund which, under the blanket of the Northern Dairies Educational Fund, supported the family for a while. I made an appeal to the Society for the Protection of Science and Learning (now called the Council for At-Risk Academics), a charity that assists foreign academics suffering political persecution. The society supported Tomin until August 1982, which was as long as their rules allowed.

After Tomin's departure, seminars similar to his were organized by other Czech philosophers, such as Ladislav Hejdánek and Petr Rezek. British philosophers such as Roger Scruton, Ralph Walker and Christopher Taylor were regular visitors under the auspices of a charitable trust, the Jan Hus Educational Foundation, set up in 1980. On one notorious occasion, the police detained the French philosopher Jacques Derrida, which brought upon the Czech authorities a personal rebuke from President Mitterrand. Philosophers from many countries continued their contacts with the dissident groups until the authorities who suppressed them were swept away in Havel's revolution. At a ceremony in Magdalen College in 1998, President Havel presented medals to several people involved with the Jan Hus foundation, including Barbara Day, who has since written a history of the whole movement under the title, *The Velvet Philosophers*.

Meanwhile, Julius remained in England, preferring to live on benefit rather than apply for any job he was likely to get. He was convinced that he was entitled to be awarded – without competition – a tenured academic post, and would accept nothing less. He was outraged when once I drew his attention to a vacancy for a librarian. From time to time he would appear outside Balliol to make a demonstration, or to parade himself on hunger strike. He fired off bitter letters of accusation and published savage articles, one of which was entitled 'Encounters with Oxford Dons'. I was one of the targets of that article, but got off not too badly: the people he attacked most bitterly were those who had done most to help him – Kathy Wilkes and Roger Scruton. At one time, an Oxford pub appointed him resident philosopher, and he would denounce to the assembled drinkers his ill treatment by the Oxford establishment.

The Tomins' marriage broke up, and their children encountered many difficulties. After Havel came to power, Julius returned for a period to Czechoslovakia, but came back to England some time later with a new wife. The tragic nature of his story is well brought out by Barbara Day in *The Velvet Philosophers*:

> The problem was not to do with his intelligence or ability, but with the lifetime spent under totalitarianism. During that time he had learnt how to be courageous, steadfast, and inspiring, but these were not

qualities listed in job descriptions for British academic posts, which required people who could work as part of a team, carry out set tasks, and act as a consistent mediator and guide for students.

# 17

## Three Irish leaders

### Charles Haughey, Taoiseach

Charley Haughey was the leader of the Fianna Fáil party, the successor to the extreme nationalist faction in the Irish Civil War of the 1920s. When I met him he was leader of the opposition to the coalition government of Garret FitzGerald (Fine Gael) and Dick Spring (Labour). As vice chair of the Kilbrandon Committee I was sent to interview him, because it was he who had insisted that in the New Ireland Forum, the unitary state – the united Ireland of tradition – should be given pride of place.

The difficulty of achieving a united Ireland by consent, he assured me, was entirely due to the intransigence of the UK government. Once that government agreed to everyone sitting around the table together, without preconditions, it would be an easy task to persuade the Unionists of the obvious merits of a unitary state governed from Dublin.

My encounter with Haughey was brief – the briefest of all the encounters recorded in this book. But it stays in my mind because on no other occasion in my life has anyone, with a straight face, told me so many lies that he knew were lies, and that he knew I knew were lies.

### Garret FitzGerald, Taoiseach

If Haughey was one of the nastiest people I have met, FitzGerald was one of the nicest. Once he realized that the Kilbrandon Committee intended to make a serious considered response to his New Ireland Forum, he was extremely helpful to me and my colleagues. He gave ample time to interview, introduced us to useful colleagues, and offered generous hospitality. His sparkling intelligence and impish wit made it always a pleasure to be in his company.

Garret was relaxed about protocol and security. Once, while giving me a lift to luncheon in the Dublin yacht club, he discussed on the telephone, *en clair*, the details of the budget he was working on with his finance minister. He loved teasing people. Once he said that it was a great pity that Ireland did not have an established Church. Since Ireland had at that time the reputation of being the most priest-ridden country in Europe, I was thoroughly startled. 'If we had an established Church', he explained, 'I would be able to appoint the bishops instead of having to put up with the people the Vatican sends us.'

His efforts to bring the British and Irish governments close together and to guarantee the rights of the Catholic minority in Northern Ireland bore fruit in 1985, with the signature of the Anglo-Irish Agreement at Hillsborough. The agreement was ratified in the Dáil by 85 votes to 75, Haughey complaining that it violated the Republic's constitution by accepting British sovereignty over part of the national territory. But public opinion in Ireland supported the agreement, and it led in the end to the repeal of the article in the constitution that laid claim to the territory of the whole island.

My final memory of Garret is of the installation of Roy Jenkins as Chancellor of Oxford University in 1987. By tradition, a new chancellor may give honorary degrees to a number of his friends on such an occasion. I was delighted that both Garret and I were among the honorands on that occasion. My wife and I were able to give useful assistance, by facing down obstructive policemen who would not allow our car close enough to the Sheldonian Theatre to allow access to Garret's disabled wife, of whom he always took the tenderest care.

## Mary Robinson, President of Ireland

One of those who helped FitzGerald draw up the proposals in the New Ireland Forum was Mary Robinson, a Belfast lawyer who was also a member of the Irish Senate. She and her colleagues drew up a careful analysis of the possibility of authority in Northern Ireland being exercised jointly by the British and Irish governments. In the event, the report of her subcommittee was not published as part of the Forum report. However, she gave sight of it to the members of the Kilbrandon Committee, and we drew on it considerably in our own proposals.

When the Hillsborough Agreement was reached, Mary and I were among those who thought that it conceded too much to the nationalists without compensating benefits to the Unionists. Because of my position in the British-Irish Association, the gist of the agreement was telephoned to me from Downing Street the day before it was published. I listened with keen interest, and then waited. 'That's fine for the nationalists', I said. 'And what are you doing for the Unionists?' There was silence. A friend of mine who was a moderate Unionist MP wrote of his reaction when the text of the agreement was handed to him: 'As I stood in the cold outside Hillsborough Castle, everything that I held dear turned to ashes in my mouth.'

While at the British-Irish Association, I made friends with a number of Unionists, notably David Trimble, who later won the Nobel Peace Prize. I regret that I never met the Revd Ian Paisley, founder of the Democratic Unionists, but I once saw and heard him. One Saturday, my wife and I were giving our weekly lunch to undergraduates in the Balliol lodgings, and we heard a voice, familiar from TV, intoning the last words of the martyred Bishop Latimer: 'Be of good comfort, Master Ridley, and play the man. We shall this day light such a candle, by God's grace, in England, as I trust shall never be put out.' When we looked out of the window, we saw Paisley standing on the spot in Broad Street where the Protestant martyrs had been burned. He was protesting against the visit of Pope John Paul II, who was at that moment touching down in Heathrow.

Ian Paisley Junior was occasionally present at British-Irish Association meetings. On one occasion, he came to see me to explain that he could not accept our invitation to dinner because he would have to sit down with ministers from the Irish Republic, and this was against his party's rules. His embarrassment was so patent, and his apology so courteous, that I concluded that he must have been very well brought up.

A few days after the Hillsborough Agreement I was in Belfast lecturing to a group of civil servants, and after the lecture I called on Mary Robinson and discovered that she shared my view that the agreement was too hard on the Unionists. In protest at its terms, she resigned her membership of the Labour Party in the Irish Senate. It was a generous gesture – one which she may well have believed would end her career in public life.

Hillsborough was an overcorrection of years of discrimination against the Catholic minority in Northern Ireland. It laid the foundation for the more balanced Good Friday agreement of 1998, which regulates the government of the province to this day. Meanwhile, Mary went on to become President of Ireland and United Nations High Commissioner for Human Rights. In recent years, I have seen her from time to time, and she came to stay with us at Rhodes House, and talk to the Rhodes Scholars. One of the wonderful things about her is that, in spite of rising to such heights, her manner has changed not a whit since we sat as young-sters together lamenting the one-sidedness of the Hillsborough Agreement over a glass of whiskey in her Belfast apartment.

# 18

# Three South African leaders

## Desmond Tutu, Archbishop of Cape Town

For some years I was a delegate of Oxford University Press, and a member of its finance committee: that is to say, I was a non-executive director of the university's publishing arm. The Press maintained, and maintains, a large branch in South Africa. During the years of apartheid, many of the OUP staff, and some of the delegates, thought the branch should be closed down, even though it was doing a valuable service in providing textbooks for black schools. Sir Roger Elliott, the chief executive, asked me to help him reach a decision whether the branch should continue to operate. We decided to seek advice from leading black South Africans.

Archbishop Tutu was in London at the time, and we paid him a visit. He was firmly in favour of closure. 'I am Mr Sanctions', he said. 'I believe that the way to end apartheid is not by the armed struggle, but by economic means. I don't care how much good you may be doing, but there can be no exceptions to the boycott.' This was clear advice. However, we telephoned Oliver Tambo, then in Scandinavia, to get a second opinion. He set the matter in the context of an academic, rather than an economic boycott, and said that we should give priority to the educational needs of the majority community. In the light of this conflicting advice, we kept the branch open, but subjected it to the scrutiny of a local committee headed by Wieland Gevers, who later became Cabinet Secretary to the Mandela government.

Tutu came to Oxford in 1990 to receive an honorary Doctor of Divinity, and I met him again in 1994 after the end of apartheid. I reminded him of our conversation about sanctions: 'I'm afraid we did not take your advice', I said. 'Quite right!', he replied. 'It was remarkably bad advice.' In fact, he said, it would have been a remarkable piece of bad timing if OUP, having operated throughout the years of the National Party government, had pulled out on the eve of a new South Africa.

I much admired the way in which Tutu, having been at the forefront of the fight against apartheid, stepped out of the limelight as soon as Mandela was freed. I have met him several times since then, and he always radiates energy and cheerfulness. He is totally lacking in pomp. And he has never set great store by decorum, whether he was publicly chastising Mandela for his delay in marrying Graça Machel, or dancing toyi-toyi in the London Guildhall with a long train of female admirers.

### Mamphela Ramphele, vice chancellor

In the 1980s, Balliol offered every year a visiting fellowship at the University of the Witwatersrand in Johannesburg. The fellowship was named after an alumnus of the college, the liberal politician Jan Hofmeyr, whom many had hoped would be the successor of Jan Smuts. At that time, the Association of University Teachers had a policy of boycotting South African academic institutions, which for a while I respected. But then I met Francis Wilson of the University of Cape Town (UCT), a South African of impeccable anti-apartheid credentials, who spent a sabbatical year in Oxford. He convinced me that the academic boycott did most damage to people in the universities who were seeking to overturn apartheid, and none at all to the authorities who upheld it.

In 1984, therefore, I accepted the Hofmeyr fellowship and travelled to South Africa with my family. Our first port of call was to the Hogsback, the rural home of Francis and his wife Lindy. It was in the midst of a forest planted by Francis' missionary grandfather, and landscaped by his mother, the anthropologist Monica Wilson. The Wilsons, there and in their house in Cape Town, introduced us to some figures in the United Democratic Front (UDF), then the main centre of resistance to government policies. Our first encounter was with the Dutch Reformed pastor Allan Boesak, one of the leaders of the UDF. Sadly, he later turned out to be a broken reed. Much better fortune followed our introduction to Mamphela Ramphele.

Mamphela had been a student activist in the Black Consciousness Movement, and had been a partner of Steve Biko, the leader of the movement, who died at the hands of the South African police. When we met, she and Francis Wilson had just jointly produced, for the Carnegie Foundation, a report on the economic consequences of apartheid. Paternalistic nationalists had argued that, though black people had no political rights in South Africa, they were better off – in terms of education, health and living standards – than the inhabitants of independent sub-Saharan states. Francis and Mamphela showed, to the contrary, that in respect of such things as infant mortality and expectation of life, South Africa's black population came near the bottom of the league table. At a dinner in our early days in Cape Town, Francis placed me next to Mamphela. She lectured me for two hours on the evils of British imperialism. It was the beginning of a long friendship.

It was after I moved to Rhodes House that Nancy and I began to see a lot of Mamphela, who stayed with us occasionally, once with her young son. In 1993, she was made chair of one of the South African Rhodes selection committees. Summing up at the end of one selection session she said that she willingly gave up a weekend at a busy time because the encounter with the candidates was such a hopeful and rejuvenating experience. 'It is indeed ironic', she said, 'that Cecil Rhodes, who epitomizes imperialism in South Africa, offered a scholarship scheme that has become a highly significant vehicle for helping to create a new kind of society at the end of the twentieth century.' In 1996 she became the first black person, and the first woman, to be appointed Vice Chancellor of the University of Cape Town.

In the latter half of the 1990s, the endowments of the Rhodes Trust regularly generated an annual surplus after all the expenses of the scholarships had been met. Now that the political climate had changed, I had no difficulty in persuading the trustees that it was appropriate to use these funds to support good causes in South Africa. Since 1973, the national officers of the trust had operated a system of bursaries for black schoolchildren, which supported more than a hundred a year. By 1995, higher-level bursaries had been added, and there were in that year 79 students holding Rhodes bursaries in attendance at UCT.

Over the decade, the trust gave over £4 million to South African causes. The largest such benefaction was announced at Mamphela's installation as vice chancellor. In the presence of President Mandela, she announced that the trust had earmarked 7 million rand for the construction of an All Africa House at the university. This was to provide a focal point for contact between the faculty of UCT, and faculty members from universities in other African countries. In 1999, I joined Mamphela for the official opening of the building. Once again she took the opportunity to offer a reinterpretation of the Rhodes legacy in the context of the new South Africa.

Since ceasing to work for the Rhodes Trust, I have seen little of Mamphela. Like many who were once supporters of the ANC, I have been saddened by the decline in the calibre of government since Nelson Mandela's death. I was sorry when I learned that Mamphela had turned down the opportunity to lead the Democratic Alliance, the most promising party of the opposition. She would have been an inspiring leader, and would have symbolized the multiracial form that the party must take if it is to compete successfully with the ANC.

## Nelson Mandela, President of South Africa

On our first visit to South Africa in 1984, Nancy and I carried in our suitcases a few recordings of a song, *Free Nelson Mandela*, that was banned in that country. We thought they would make useful hostess presents. In fact, we found that every house we visited already had a copy – and often several copies – smuggled in by previous visitors from the UK.

The first time we ever saw Mandela was not in South Africa but in Norway. In November 1993 I was invited to give a series of lectures in philosophy at the University of Oslo. It turned out that Mandela and F. W. de Klerk were jointly due to receive the Nobel Peace

Prize. Because my host and I were both fellows of the Norwegian Academy, we were entitled to be present at the ceremony at which the king awarded the prize. It was a great honour to be present when the prize was awarded to two such recipients who had each worked hard to bring peace within their troubled country.

I met Mandela several times later, but only on ceremonial occasions and for brief party conversations. But even the shortest time in his presence was enough to impress one with his immense affability and complete lack of bitterness. After I ceased to be secretary of the Rhodes Trust, the trustees set up, alongside the Rhodes Scholarships, a set of Mandela Rhodes Scholarships. This was due to an imaginative initiative of my successor as secretary, but above all it was an expression of Mandela's magnanimity in allowing his name to be linked with that of Rhodes. It was hoped at the time that this would purge the name of Rhodes and shield it from the obloquy hurled at it by many black South Africans. Sadly, a decade or more later, that hope proved vain.

My most picturesque memory of Mandela dates from 1997. Oxford University wished to offer him an honorary degree. When his office was approached, we learned that a dozen other British universities wished to do the same. The new President of South Africa could hardly be asked to make an academic peregrination around the country, so it was arranged that there should be a ceremony in Buckingham Palace at which representatives of the various universities should make their laudations and present their scrolls to the honorand. I was a member of the Oxford delegation.

The event was a spectacular exhibition of imperialism in reverse. On the dais, beside the Duke of Edinburgh, stood Nelson Mandela, handsomely attired in a plain Armani business outfit. Surrounding him were little groups of academics wearing the quaint old-fashioned dresses of their separate tribes. On approaching the dais, each vice chancellor was accompanied by a bodyguard of bedels bearing traditional weapons of truncheons and maces. I wish I could have seen the expression on the face of Queen Victoria, wherever she may now be.

# 19

## Three novelists

### Graham Greene

When Graham Greene was an undergraduate at Balliol, in the early 1920s, he was an unhappy and unruly student, not well regarded by his tutors, and he would have to get drunk in order to face his termly interview with the Master. By the time I met him he had become an honorary fellow of the college, having achieved international fame as a novelist. In 1979, Oxford University made him an honorary Doctor of Letters at Encaenia, and the college feasted him beforehand. As Master, I had the pleasure of entertaining him at the very table at which he had once had to be propped up to face handshaking. Where Oxford led, the nation followed, and in 1982 Greene was awarded the Order of Merit.

At the luncheon the day before Encaenia, Greene made a remark which had a lasting effect on my life. Greene and myself, and another guest, the Oxford publisher Dan Davin, were all, to varying degrees, lapsed Catholics. The conversation turned to the following question. Since, to the unbeliever, faith is only a delusion, why do those who have given up their faith feel a sense of loss? Greene quoted the words:

> Of all the creatures under heaven's wide cope
> We are most hopeless who had once most hope,
> We are most wretched that had most believed.

I did not recognize the quotation and was told it came from *Easter Day* by Arthur Hugh Clough. At that time, I knew of Clough only the two poems that everyone knows – *The Latest Decalogue* and *Say not the Struggle naught Availeth* – but Oxford University Press had just published the canonical edition of Clough's poems, and a day or two later Davin sent me a copy as a present. The volume soon became one of my favourites, and I spent many hours reading

Clough's poems. I particularly liked his two novels in verse, *The Bothie of Tober-na-Vuolich* about a Scottish reading party, and *Amours de Voyage* about the ineffective lovemaking of an Oxford don in the Rome of Mazzini's 1848 Republic.

For years to come, reading and writing about Clough became one of my main intellectual interests. In 1998 I wrote a book, *God and Two Poets*, in which I compared Clough's religious poetry with that of Gerard Manley Hopkins. Two years later I published an edited version of Clough's Oxford diaries, which had turned up serendipitously in Balliol library while I was researching for the earlier book. When the new *Dictionary of National Biography* appeared, I was invited to contribute the relevant article, and in 2005 I published a full-length biography of Clough. Finally, I produced an edition of Clough's lesser known poems, *Mari Magno* and *Dipsychus*. Every time I return to work on Clough I am grateful to Grahame Greene for introducing me to him.

A few years later I asked Greene to make a benefaction to Balliol. He declined, but suggested that the college should hold an auction at Christie's of items donated by old members. He promised to set the ball rolling by giving some of his own manuscripts. Sadly, they proved disappointing – typescripts of four-page introductions to reprints of his works, and the like. Now, years after his death, the college has come into possession of a full collection of Greene memorabilia, which is one of the treasures of its archives.

## Iris Murdoch

It was Elizabeth Anscombe, I believe, who introduced me to Iris Murdoch. The two of them, along with Mary Midgley and Philippa Foot, constituted a formidable group of female philosophers in Oxford in the late forties and early fifties. While Elizabeth was teaching ancient philosophy at Somerville, Iris was teaching modern philosophy at St Anne's. The two women did not, however, chime together philosophically. Iris once wrote in her diary: 'The ruthless authenticity of Elizabeth makes me feel more and more ashamed of the vague and self-indulgent way in which I have been philosophising.' Elizabeth, when she spoke to me about Iris, would adopt a tone of half-amused contempt. Relations between the two had been strained for reasons other than philosophical. Iris had been thrown out of her lodgings because of the terrible mess that Elizabeth had made there during Iris' absence. Elizabeth had been doing cooking experiments with the logician Georg Kreisel, in the course of which a chiffon scarf of Iris' had been ruined by being used to filter fish soup.

By the time I got to know Iris she had ceased to be a teacher of philosophy and had devoted herself full time to writing. I had read her early novels – *Under the Net*, *The Flight from the Enchanter*, *The Sandcastle* and *The Bell* – with great admiration. Iris retained an interest in philosophy, writing a book on Sartre in 1953. From time to time, she and I would discuss philosophy together. We shared a dislike for the neo-Kantian morality taught at that time by Richard Hare, and were both to some extent outside the mainstream of Oxford philosophy – she with her initial fascination with existentialism, and I with my scholastic background. I tried to persuade her that we should conduct a seminar together, but she refused to be drawn back into academic philosophy. Instead, she continued to publish philosophical books such as *The Sovereignty of Good*, and *Metaphysics as a Guide to Morals*. For an Aristotelian like myself her works were far too Platonic.

My wife and I had an opportunity to sample the hospitality of Iris and her husband John Bayley. The challenges of their food have been well described by other writers, but I have a more vivid memory of our hosts' attitude to wine. 'Never acquire a taste for fine wine', Iris warned us solemnly. But along with a contempt for quality, Iris and John had a great appreciation for quantity: bottle after bottle of cheap Beaujolais would be opened. The couple had no objection to the blending of wines, even accepting the mingling of white and red to form a murky rosé.

I found it dangerous to discuss with Iris any of my activities with the British-Irish Association. She came from an Irish Protestant background and had a hatred of popery, which gave her a kinship with the Ulster Unionists. This can be sensed in the background of her novel *The Red and the Green*. As the years went by, and she published novel after novel – notably *The Sea, the Sea*, which won the Booker Prize in 1978 – I lost my initial enthusiasm for her fiction, and indeed I found several of her later novels unreadable.

My last memory of Iris was of the occasion when we invited her to Rhodes House to be a dinner guest and give an after-dinner talk to the Rhodes Scholars. She was extraordinarily kind to them, taking seriously every question, whether sensible or idiotic, and encouraging would-be novelists among the Scholars, even offering to read their drafts. She had an ability, second only to that of Bill Clinton, to concentrate totally on whoever she was talking to, never looking over anyone's shoulder to see who else was around.

On the basis of my personal knowledge of her, I always regarded Iris as one of the most kind-hearted people I knew. I was saddened when, after her death, her biographers and her letters revealed another side. During her life she must have caused a great deal of pain to each of her lovers as she dumped one for another in a seemingly interminable series.

## David Lodge

Graham Greene made his name in the literary world with a series of novels with Catholic themes: *Brighton Rock*, with its teenage gangster, *The Power and the Glory*, with its whisky priest, and *The End of the Affair*, which inserts a miraculous element into a love story. David Lodge, in his autobiography, records that when he was a teenage Catholic with aspirations to be a writer, it was encouraging and inspiring that the two most famous English literary novelists living in the forties and fifties were both Catholics writing of Catholic themes. In the minds of many young Catholic readers, Graham Greene was paired with Evelyn Waugh.

I do not know David Lodge at all well: we meet from time to time at parties and at seminars. But I include him among these memoirs because his novels have captured in accurate detail the background to the various stages of my life. I never had to do national service, so his 1962 novel *Ginger, You're Barmy* passed me by. But *The British Museum is Falling Down* (1965) dealt with an issue which constantly cropped up in my dealings with parishioners while I was a curate in the early sixties. This was the 'rhythm method' of contraception, which was the form recommended by the Catholic Church. Many people felt that since the intention in each case was to avoid conceiving a baby, it was hypocritical to make a moral distinction between the use of the safe period (permitted) and the use of condoms (forbidden). I recall Peter Geach defending the Catholic position by pointing out that there was a difference between fixing the date of a college meeting on a day when an obnoxious fellow was likely to be absent, and shutting the door in his face on a day when he turned up. David Lodge, who had himself suffered from the unreliability of the rhythm method, turned it in the novel into black comedy. In its first chapter, the hero's wife is shown lying in bed with so many thermometers sticking out of her that she resembles a hedgehog on heat.

*How Far Can You Go?* (1980) takes as its title a question I was frequently asked when I was an assistant chaplain at Oxford. Premarital intercourse was impossible for an observant Catholic pair – but short of copulation, they would ask, what other forms of endearment were allowed? The devout young would inquire about the permissible limits of 'heavy petting', as it was then called. From my own experience of annual meetings of university Cath. Socs, I could call up acquaintances to replicate each of the characters in Lodge's book. One character was a striking match for a friend of mine who was a devout daily Mass-goer. He always mapped out the day's liturgy with seven multicoloured ribbons in his missal. Like the character in the novel, my friend eventually came out of the closet as a homosexual.

When I moved into an academic career, Lodge was always there waiting with a novel to describe my new environment. In *Changing Places*, the hero, Philip Sparrow, travels from the University of

Rummidge to Euphoric State University in California, while his American opposite number Morris Zapp crosses the Atlantic in the opposite direction. I read and reread this book as I took visiting professorships in Chicago, Seattle, Stanford, Michigan, Minnesota and Cornell. Sadly, I never spent more than a few days at Berkeley, the archetype of Euphoric State, but I have met more than one Professor Zapp in the course of my travels. To this day, the best passages in the novel, when I read them for the fourth or fifth time, make me laugh aloud.

As I have grown old I have come to enjoy reading Lodge's novels more than those of his heroes Greene and Waugh. I prefer his ironic realism also to the metaphysical flights of the later Murdoch. His novels continue to offer vignettes of new features of my life. When we moved into Rhodes House, my wife and I were surprised to discover that we had in our garden a family of foxes. Here is Lodge's hero, Vic, in *Nice Work*:

> One morning not long ago he saw a fox walking past his window. Vic tapped on the pane. The fox stopped and turned his head to look at Vic for a moment, as if to say *Yes?* and then proceeded calmly on his way, his brush swaying in the air behind him. It is Vic's impression that English wildlife is getting streetwise, moving from the country into the city where life is easier – where there are no traps, pesticides, hunters and sportsmen, but plenty of well-stocked garbage bins.

Finally, *Deaf Sentence* was published just in time to greet my own loss of hearing. Like the hero of that novel, I have found that my hearing aid can be surprisingly creative. One morning recently I came downstairs and said to my wife, 'Did you hear that an Oxford historian has been found guilty of murder?' We spent a fascinating breakfast speculating which of our colleagues was the murderer, and who had been his victim. We could not, however, find a totally convincing answer, and eventually Nancy asked me, 'Is it possible that what you heard was "Oscar Pistorius convicted of murder"?'

I have not read the 2004 *Author, Author*, a fiction based on the life of Henry James, which was embarrassingly pipped to the post by another book on the same topic by Colm Tóibín. But I look forward to David's next novel, which will no doubt describe exactly what it is like to be on one's last legs.

# 20

# Three scientists

## Noam Chomsky, linguist

Unsurprisingly, the scientists I have got to know in my academic career have all been people who worked on the border between science and philosophy. Such was Noam Chomsky. He was the most celebrated linguist of the twentieth century, and continues to be influential in that discipline. But his work has always interested philosophers as well as linguists. From a philosophical point of view, he can be best located in relation to the teaching of Descartes. Descartes, unlike his empiricist contemporaries, believed in innate ideas. Chomsky's position – initially at least – was similar: he argued that the swift mastery of language by children can only be explained on the basis of a species-specific human ability. The human mind, he claimed, innately possesses certain organizing principles of universal grammar as an abstract system underlying behaviour. Chomsky made popular the notion of *faculty*, and gave it an import-ance that it had not had in psychology for centuries. In this he was at the opposite pole from Descartes, who regarded the notion of faculties as an Aristotelian anachronism that stood in the way of genuine scientific progress.

I first engaged academically with Chomsky when I reviewed, in *Philosophical Transactions of the Royal Society*, his 1980 book, *Rules and Representations*. I found no difficulty in principle with the postulation of innate mental structures, nor with the notion of faculties. Obviously, human beings are born with certain capacities, including capacities to mature as well as capacities to learn. Whether the capacity to acquire grammars of a certain kind is a capacity for learning, or a capacity for maturation, seemed to me a philosoph-ically open question, capable of being settled by empirical inquiry. So far I was with Chomsky, but in my review I went on to claim that his overall philosophy of mind was confused: it became impossible at some points to tell whether he was talking about mental software or about neurological hardware. As time went on, I began to think that Chomsky the philosopher was getting in the way of Chomsky the linguist.

I cannot remember when I first met Noam personally, but I do recall a set of lectures that he came from MIT to give in Oxford in the 1980s – lectures that were always packed out by throngs of both junior and senior members. During question time he was immensely courteous, speaking in a passionless monotone. He had the gift of turning the most fatuous question into a serious query, to be given a precise answer; and he displayed the same character-istics when we corresponded with each other across the Atlantic. Some months could pass before a response came to a criticism of mine. Then a letter would arrive: 'Unless you have the memory of an elephant you will have forgotten that you said . . .' – followed by a meticulous point-by-point response.

I have never seriously studied Noam's political writings, and some of his political conclusions seem to me so implausible that I have been disinclined to study his evidence, even if I were competent to evaluate it. I find his neo-anarchism incredible as a policy. But on one political issue I think he is completely right: that during the Cold War and its aftermath, US foreign policy has been no less disastrous than that of the USSR and its successors. Throughout my life I have spoken in this sense. During the Cuban Missile Crisis, while still a curate, I got into trouble for preaching a sermon that complained that Khrushchev and Kennedy were two equally evil men who were threatening civilization with destruction. In 1986, I spoke at an Oxford Union debate against Richard Perle, then US Assistant Secretary of Defense, arguing that the Reagan administra-tion's defence policies were making the world less, rather than more, safe. Finally, when Tony Blair led the UK to follow the USA into war in Iraq, I marched with a million other UK citizens in protest.

Meghan Markle, the latest royal duchess since her marriage to Prince Harry, is a keen reader of Chomsky. She has recom-mended his *Who Rules the World?* to her multitudinous followers on

Instagram. Noam is reported to have said that it sounds as though she may 'shake up the royal family'.

The last time that I saw Noam was when he visited Rhodes House and addressed a group of Rhodes Scholars. The American ones were more interested in his radical political views than in his linguistic theories. During the discussion he made the most outrageous statements in the same flat voice that he used to expound finer points of linguistics. At breakfast the following morning, he did his best to persuade my wife and myself that the only person, other than himself, whose political judgement could be relied on was the then reigning pope, John Paul II. Only the pope, he said, realized that American capitalism was every bit as wicked as Soviet communism had ever been.

## Richard Dawkins, atheist biologist

Richard Dawkins and I have been Oxford colleagues for most of our lives, and have been sparring with each other for many years. We agree with each other that most of what religious people believe is false, but unlike Richard I accept that religious beliefs may be quite reasonable, even if untrue. While I am not competent to challenge any of Richard's scientific statements, and while I regard his *The Extended Phenotype* as one of the last century's finest books of popular science, I believe that he greatly exaggerates the power of genetics to explain human life and thought. We first clashed in a seminar at Holywell Manor, chaired by Denis Noble, shortly after *The Selfish Gene* appeared. Richard thought that now the DNA code had been cracked, we would be able to understand the book of life. 'Do you think that a knowledge of the English alphabet is all you need to understand Shakespeare?', I asked him.

When I read *The God Delusion* I found I agreed with about 90 per cent of what it said, but that the area of disagreement meant that the two of us came to quite different positions about the rationality of religious belief. I will mention just one example. I am an agnostic about the existence of God, whereas Richard is an atheist and believes that he can prove that God certainly does not exist. A designer God, he maintains, cannot be used to explain the organized complexity we observe in living beings, because any God capable of designing anything would have to be complex enough to demand the same kind of explanation in his own right. He calls this argument 'The Ultimate Boeing 747 gambit', in tribute to Fred Hoyle, who once said that the probability of life originating on earth is no greater than the chance that a hurricane, sweeping through a scrapyard, would have the luck to assemble a Boeing 747. God, according to Dawkins, is the ultimate 747.

A traditional theist would say that Dawkins' argument misrepresented the notion of God in two ways. First of all, God is as much outside the series complexity/simplicity as he is outside the series mover/moved. He is not complex as a protein is; nor, for that matter, is he simple as an elementary particle is. He has neither the simplicity nor the complexity of material objects. Second, he is not one of a series of temporal contingents, each requiring explanation in terms of a previous state of the universe: unchanging and everlasting, he is outside the temporal series. What calls for explanation is the origin of organized complexity: but God had no origin, and is neither complex nor organized.

I made this point in a lecture to the Royal Institute of Philosophy in 2007. A few years later I was asked to take part in a debate, in Oxford's Sheldonian Theatre, between Richard and the Archbishop of Canterbury, Rowan Williams. The topic of the debate was 'the nature of human beings and their ultimate origin'. As an agnostic, I was supposed to be a neutral chair holding the balance between the Christian and an atheist. But as the debate proceeded I began to think that the kindly archbishop was letting Richard get away with some pretty feeble arguments, and so I began to intervene on the other side. When Richard again produced his Boeing 747 argument, I protested that he was confusing two kinds of complexity – complexity of structure and complexity of function. A cut-throat razor was a much simpler structure than an electric shaver, but unlike the shaver it could also function as a cut-throat as well as a razor. The archbishop, fingering his beard, said that he did not feel competent to adjudicate between us.

Richard and I have always got on amicably face to face, but have not been afraid to be rude to each other in absence or in print. At dinner, after the Sheldonian debate, I remarked to Richard that moving from *The Extended Phenotype* to *The God Delusion* was like moving from the *Financial Times* to *The Sun*. This did not go down well, and led to a frosty exchange of emails. Later, Richard took part in a debate in Sydney with Cardinal Pell. At some point in the debate, I am told, the cardinal referred to my critique of the argument for atheism: 'Ah, Kenny', Richard said. 'He is a qualified obscurantist.' Well, I do have a doctorate in theology, which I suppose from Richard's point of view is a professional qualification in obscurantism.

## Denis Noble, biologist

When I was a bachelor don at Balliol I shared a staircase with Denis Noble, who was a physiology tutor: my rooms were on one side of the staircase and his on the other. We were both courting at the time, and so would also meet each other's fiancées on the stairs. We shared students as well as premises. There was an honour school called PPP: Psychology, Philosophy and Physiology. Denis taught the students physiology and I taught them philosophy. At meals in college we often discussed topics of common interest: Denis was not only a physiologist but as competent a philosopher as any of my colleagues.

In those days, there was a broad consensus that the sciences formed a hierarchy in which each level was to be explained in terms of the one below it: psychology was to be explained by physiology, physiology by chemistry, and chemistry by physics. This scientific strategy was called 'reductionism', since all sciences were ultimately to be reduced to physics. The idea was pithily expressed by Jim Watson, one of the discoverers of DNA: 'There are only molecules – everything else is sociology.'

Reductionist science chalked up victory after victory, as more and more lower-level mechanisms were discovered to explain higher-level processes. One such discovery was made in 1984 by the young Denis. He explained the pacemaker rhythm of the heart in terms of the flow of ions of potassium and calcium through protein channels. This achievement established his credentials as a reductionist biologist. However, he did not long continue to be a card-carrying member of the fraternity. He soon realized that in the heartbeat there was not only upward causation from the molecular level to the cellular level, but also downward causation from the cell influencing the molecules. Denis chaired the meeting at which I challenged Dawkins on the explanatory power of genes, and he took my side in the argument.

After I became Master of the college I ceased to share students with Denis, and so we had less opportunity for scientific discussion. However, our paths remained entwined at an administrative level. For two years, Denis served as my vice Master. This period included the year in which Mrs Thatcher was proposed, and then rejected, for an honorary Oxford degree. Denis was a founder of the Save British Science campaign which protested against the Thatcher government's cuts to the science budget, and he took a leading part in the campaign against the proposal. After the proposal was rejected, 200 alumni wrote separate letters to Balliol, either to applaud or to condemn the decision of Congregation. Denis and I divided between us the burden of replying. I, who had voted in Council in favour of the degree, wrote to the pro-Thatcher correspondents, while Denis wrote to the rest.

In retirement, I have been delighted to resume philosophical and scientific discussions with Denis. He has now come a long way from his reductionist beginnings. In his latest book, *Dance to the Tune of Life*, he enunciates a principle that he calls 'biological relativity'. This states that in biology there is no privileged level of causation: living organisms are multilevel open systems in which the behaviour at any level depends on higher and lower levels, and cannot be fully understood in isolation. Levels are distinguished from each other by their degree of complexity. If we start with atoms, we move upward through the levels of molecules, networks, organelles, cells, tissues, organs, whole-body systems and whole organisms.

One of the goals of reductionism was to eliminate from science all teleology or goal-directedness. In fact, Noble argues, teleology is ubiquitous in nature. However, it operates in different ways at different levels. At the purely molecular level, the protein-membrane network that sustains cardiac rhythm has no goal: its function only becomes clear at the level of cells. In its turn, the cellular activity serves a purpose that only emerges at the still higher level of the cardiovascular system.

While he remains a thoroughgoing Darwinist, Denis challenges the neo-Darwinism of Dawkins. He rejects the assumption that natural selection working on chance variations in genetic material is entirely sufficient to explain all evolutionary change, and has followed up the critique of *The Selfish Gene* that we began in his Holywell Manor drawing room years ago. In *Dance to the Tune of Life*, he argues that genes are not agents – selfish or unselfish: they are only templates – mere organs of the living cell:

> There is nothing alive in the DNA molecule alone. If I could completely isolate a whole genome, put it in a Petri dish with as many nutrients as we may wish, I could keep it for 10,000 years and it would do absolutely nothing other than to slowly degrade.

Moreover, DNA is not sealed off from the outside world: it is subject to modification from within the organism and from the environment. Human beings and other animals are not lumbering robots but autonomous agents who can affect not only their environment but also the make-up of their own genome.

In 2017, Denis organized a joint conference between the Royal Society and the British Academy on the new trends in evolutionary biology. Despite attempts made to block it by outraged neo-Darwinists, the conference was well attended and excited all the participants. I am proud to have had a hand in the early stages of its organization. Its proceedings have recently been published by the Royal Society in its journal *Interface Focus*.

To this day, Denis and I continue our discussions on the relationship between philosophy and science. We both agree that the notion that science is necessarily and uniquely reductionist is not an empirical discovery, but a philosophical postulate. We both agree that teleology is undeniable and ubiquitous, but that we do not know, and perhaps cannot know, whether this is simply a fundamental feature of nature, or whether there is some supreme level at which it has an explanation. Certainly science cannot tell us whence the universe originated, and whether it has an ultimate goal. In his latest book, Denis suggests that even in asking these questions we have reached a boundary across which we cannot go.